The Inside Story
of the Teacher Revolution
in America

Don Cameron

ScarecrowEducation
Lanham, Maryland • Toronto • Oxford
2005

Published in the United States of America
by ScarecrowEducation
An imprint of The Rowman & Littlefield Publishing Group, Inc.
4501 Forbes Boulevard, Suite 200, Lanham, Maryland 20706
www.scaroweducation.com

PO Box 317
Oxford
OX2 9RU, UK

British Library Cataloguing in Publication Information Available

Library of Congress Cataloging-in-Publication Data

Cameron, Don Roland, 1937–
  The inside story of the teacher revolution in America / Don Roland
Cameron.
      p. cm.
  Includes index.
  ISBN 1-57886-196-9 (pbk. : alk. paper)
  1. Teachers' unions—United States—History—20th century. 2.
Teachers—Professional relationships—United States. I. Title.
LB2844.53.U6C36 2005
371.1'00973—dc22   2004019439

∞™ The paper used in this publication meets the minimum requirements of
American National Standard for Information Sciences—Permanence of
Paper for Printed Library Materials, ANSI/NISO Z39.48-1992.
Manufactured in the United States of America.

This book is dedicated to the teachers of America, and to one in particular: Ida Jane Arcand Cameron, who taught me what love, dedication, and courage are all about. It is also dedicated to Amanda and Benjamin, our remarkable children.

Contents

Preface

This book is my personal account of the teacher revolution of the 1960s and '70s. Why did teachers unionize? What compelled them to abandon their passive way of life and embrace militancy and collective bargaining? Who or what was responsible for their sudden turn toward confrontation? What role did teacher unions play in that turn? Were America's classroom teachers unwillingly forced into unions or were they eager participants?

The answers to those questions and many more can be found only in the context of how America has traditionally treated its public school teachers. That context is central to the story. Since well before the Civil War, teachers in our nation's public schools have given of themselves diligently, unselfishly, and competently to the causes of education and democracy. Without their considerable professionalism, an educated citizenry would never have been possible. In spite of that, public school teachers have never been afforded the credit or recognition they richly deserve. Most Americans don't recognize just how good their country's teachers are. This account is written on behalf of those teachers; hopefully, it will meet with their approval.

Militant teachers didn't suddenly emerge from alien pods that germinated in school boiler rooms. Neither were they created by a bunch of greedy union bosses in smoke-filled union halls. Militant teachers were the inevitable product of an oppressive environment under which they had labored for generations, unappreciated and underpaid. When the situation became professionally unbearable, they revolted. This is the story of that revolution told by someone who experienced from the inside. More specifically, it's about the courageous men and women of the National Education Association (NEA) as well as those of the American Federation of Teachers (AFT).

This book is not a history of NEA or of American education. It is simply a firsthand account of my forty years spent in the education vineyards as a teacher; association member; elected leader; negotiator; and staffer at the local, state, and national levels. My experiences and observations as a participant in the revolution and its forty-year aftermath are chronicled here, including my tenure as executive director of the National Education Association. I now enjoy the luxury of speaking as a private citizen without the constraints of NEA policy or politics; and my opinions and observations, however imperfect, are set forth here. I am responsible for any and all factual inaccuracies.

This book is about the struggle of teachers for survival within their chosen profession, a struggle they have been waging for over two hundred years. Teachers take great pride in their efforts to educate America's students. William Butler Yeats, the renowned Irish poet and playwright, wrote: "Teaching is not the filling of a pail, but the lighting of a fire." Lighting fires of intellectual curiosity is really what teaching is all about, and America's educators light those fires every day in the young minds they teach. Lighting fires is, after all, what teachers do. It's who they are.

When I taught seventh grade in Michigan back in the '60s, I was handed a handwritten letter at the end of the year by one of my students, a bright but edgy kid. He said, "Mr. Cameron, this is from the class; read it when you get home." I did.

Dear Mr. Cameron:
In the short months that we have known you, we have gained a little bit of the meaning of life. Your class is the best we've ever had. Your weird sense of humor and the almost comical way you get us to learn should be put in a book and given to all teachers at the beginning of the year, entitled "How to teach a class of hoodlums and get them to learn." That's all for now, but I'm sure we'll see you in the halls next year walking at that breakneck speed of yours (ha! ha!). Thanks for making our education so meaningful and rewarding.

Every member of the class signed the letter, and four decades later it still brings me joy. Sometimes, when I'm feeling a little down, it gets dragged out and reread. All good teachers have similar letters or comments stashed away in their memory banks. Classroom souvenirs like this one do much more than define teachers' effectiveness; they define their worth. I want to share with the readers of this book at least some of the passion that teachers feel for educating kids, because through the Sturm und Drang of teacher advocacy over the last forty years, they grafted that passion onto my soul.

However, in the 1960s teachers collectively lit a fire of a different kind. It was a fire they set within the education and political establishment, and it precipitated a revolution of far-reaching consequence. It set ablaze the professional prison that had confined them over the previous century. The dictionary defines revolution as "any fundamental change or reversal of conditions," and what America's teachers underwent during that period certainly fits the definition. While countless numbers of books have been written about teacher unions and education reform, the inside story of the teacher revolution and its impact on education generally, and on the National Education Association in particular, has gone largely untold.

In the forty-year period from 1962 to 2002, America experienced tremendous social and political turmoil on a variety of fronts: the civil rights movement; the assassination of some of the country's greatest and most inspirational leaders; the fight for equality for women; the movement to secure equity for gays and lesbians; the transformational change in the American economy and workplace, including the rapid advance of computers and technology; the dismantling of the Berlin Wall and the breakup of the Soviet Union; the placing of a man on the moon and robots on Mars; three full-fledged wars and assorted military invasions; the largest influx of immigrants to our shores in American history; and, of course, the mind-bending horror of international terrorism.

During that same time frame, tectonic changes occurred within education: the passage of state collective-bargaining statutes for public employees in the '60s and '70s; the rapid expansion of teacher unionism (by the new millennia, NEA had become the nation's largest and most powerful organization of public employees with a membership of 2.6 million and an annual budget of $225 million); the rise of teacher political activism; the release of the *Nation at Risk* report in 1983 and the drive for education reform that followed; the tremendous impact of technology on teachers and students; the controversy over bilingual education; the largely ridiculous debate over phonics vs. whole language in the teaching of reading; the school choice and privatization movements; incessant attacks on public education by ultraconservative ideologues; the federal government's yo-yo effect on public-education funding caused by frequent shifts in political philosophies; and the much-needed standards movement and its unintended obsession with high-stakes standardized tests.

Those forty years, including the teacher revolution, coincided almost precisely with my own career in education. In the 1960s, collective bargaining for teachers created an organizational tsunami that forced the National Education Association and its affiliates to become advocates for school employees. That NEA transformation is of no small consequence, because prior to that time the association had occupied a highly respected and cozy catbird seat within the education establishment. Its respect within education and political circles was surpassed only by its ineffectiveness in raising the salaries of teachers or improving their working conditions.

The roots of the 1960s revolution that turned NEA upside down are buried deep within the history of public education in America and its culture of teacher powerlessness. For over a century, America's teachers were required to be compliant, quiet, and "professional." They had been forced to work for little remuneration under conditions ranging from barely adequate to abject squalor. For over a century, just beneath education's deceptively tranquil surface, teacher frustrations over the twin scourges of low pay and patronization had been growing increasingly unstable.

When state collective-bargaining statutes for public employees finally became a reality in the 1960s, long-dormant teacher frustrations erupted, unleashing a fury that surprised most people, including many educators. From Maine to California, teachers with a long history of submissiveness and acquiescence set their jaws and started making demands. They used collective bargaining as their vehicle for equity and respect like shipwrecked sailors clinging to driftwood to transport them ashore. In adopting collective bargaining and unionism, teachers jettisoned long-standing but unproductive relationships with school admin-

istrators and school boards, the old "education family" that had inef-
fectually embraced them for generations. They also announced to an
apathetic public that they would no longer be taken for granted, and
they meant it.

I jumped on board the union train when it passed through Birmingham, Michigan, in the summer of 1965 and never looked back. During
my long journey, years and events sped past like telephone poles
whizzing by a train window. Along the way, the union train deposited
me in the middle of a whirlwind of memorable events and movements,
making sure that I got to the right places at the right time. I did just
about everything a teacher advocate can do: taught school; joined the
association; organized members; negotiated contracts; served as an
elected teacher leader; and worked on staff at all levels of the organization's structure (local, state, and national).

I worked in the areas of organizing, collective bargaining, public relations, political action, and association management, and served as an
executive manager for teacher unions in Michigan, Florida, and Washington, D.C. Over the years I knew and worked directly with literally
tens of thousands of teachers and other school personnel, and inter-
acted with school-board members, school administrators, mayors,
governors, state legislators, members of Congress, U.S. secretaries of
education, university officials, corporation CEOs, presidents of the
United States, and education and political leaders from countries all
over the world.

On top of all that, I participated in the intense and often bitter organizational rivalry between NEA and its main competitor, the American
Federation of Teachers. Then, in the 1990s, I was proud to help lead the
two rival organizations toward rapprochement, playing a central role in
an unsuccessful national merger effort in the 1990s. The merger attempt, addressed later in the book, failed—but it did signal an end to
all-out, cutthroat competition between the two organizations. Before
retiring as NEA executive director, I participated in the pervasive and
lengthy education reform movement that followed the 1983 *Nation at
Risk* report.

My career train ride was a good, long one. There aren't many people who can honestly say that during their careers they enjoyed going
to work virtually every day in every job they had. I can. I believed that

teacher advocacy was a noble cause and that my contribution to the betterment of education generally, and of the lives of American school employees specifically, made a difference, however small. The journey provided splendid colleagues who were important to me; I enjoyed their professional companionship a great deal.

Those colleagues and I shared many hard times and faced a multitude of difficult obstacles together, but we also shared thousands of rewarding experiences and a ton of laughter. A sense of humor softens hard edges and often allows people to get past difficult situations, particularly during contract negotiations. Having said that, most jokes leave me a little cold. I'd much rather create levity by offering a humorous quip or comment about something as it is happening rather than telling a "Did you hear the one about the guy who went into a bar with a duck under his arm" kind of joke.

One story, however, always tickled me to the point that I felt compelled to share it with anyone who would listen, willingly or unwillingly. I've told the joke in every state and in many countries, and I can objectively certify that it's funny in every language. I told the joke over and over and over, always eliciting groans at the start from those who had heard it several times before. Captive audiences were my specialty. During the merger discussions with AFT, its leaders accused me of advocating the merger only because it would give me a new audience for the joke of 16 million or so AFL-CIO members. I resent that characterization. I don't deny it; I just resent it. I'm going to tell that story now because I know you want to hear it.

There was a cloistered convent where the resident nuns were allowed to say only two words every ten years. A young novitiate entered the convent, and after the first ten years passed, the Mother Superior knocks on her door and says: "My child, you've been here ten years and you are now allowed to say your first two words. What would you like to say?"

The nun replies, "Bed hard!"

Ten years later, the Mother Superior knocks on the nun's cell door and says, "My child, you've now been here twenty years, and you can say two more words. What would those two words be?"

The nun replies, "Food bad"!

After thirty years, the Mother Superior enters the nun's room and says, "OK, Sister, what do you have to say this time?"

The nun replies, "I quit!"

The Mother Superior says, "Good. All you've done is bitch ever since you got here."

Acknowledgments

In writing this book, many people helped me sharpen recollections, check facts, or round out events and stories. Most not only contributed their time and perspectives, but also gave their friendship. However, in so doing, they didn't necessarily endorse my views or bellicosity. I am very grateful to all of them, but especially the following:

- Herb Berg, Superintendent of Schools, Camden, SC
- Anne Bryant, Executive Director, National School Boards Association
- Susan Lowell Butler, former NEA Director of Communications and author of *The National Education Association—A Special Mission*
- Dave Cameron, businessman and brother
- Bob Chanin, General Counsel, National Education Association
- Bob Chase, former President, National Education Association
- John Dunlop, former Director of Negotiations, National Education Association
- Escambia Education Association (EEA), Pensacola, FL
- Sandy Feldman, President, American Federation of Teachers (AFT)
- Mary Futrell, former President, National Education Association; Dean, Graduate School of Education, George Washington University
- Keith Geiger, former President, National Education Association
- Marge Head, former President, Broward County Classroom Teachers Association (FL)
- Terry Herndon, former Executive Director, National Education Association

- Ruth Holmes, former State President, FTP-NEA (FL)
- Katie Keats, former staff member, Fairfax Education Association
- Phil Kiels, retired Michigan teacher
- Tom Koerner, ScarecrowEducation
- Irma Kramer, former Assistant Executive Director for Governance and Policy, National Education Association
- Bill Martin, former Director of Communications, National Education Association
- Ken Melley, former Assistant Executive Director for Political Affairs, National Education Association
- Ed McElroy, President, American Federation of Teachers (AFT)
- Dan McKillip, former Regional Director, National Education Association; former Executive Director, NYEA (NY)
- Judith Renyi, former Executive Director, the NEA Foundation
- NEA Research Division
- Peter Ross, retired businessman and investment counselor
- John Ryor, former President, National Education Association
- Dennis Van Roekel, Vice President, National Education Association
- Edgar B. Wesley, author of *NEA: The First Hundred Years*
- Allan West, former Associate Executive Secretary, National Education Association, and author of *The National Education Association: The Power Base for Education*
- Rick Willis, former Uniserv Director, Fairfax Education Association

CHAPTER 1

Taking Public Education for Granted

Why aren't public schools held in higher esteem than they are? After all, nine of every ten Americans are graduates of this country's public schools. Public school graduates fill the ranks of America's scientists, railway workers, astronauts, doctors, diplomats, lawyers, entertainers, politicians, and everything else. Given the vast ethnic, racial, and cultural diversity within America's population, and given the wide disparity between the very rich and the very poor, the accomplishments of public education are nothing short of phenomenal. Top American students measure up exceedingly well against students from all other countries; and America, in addition to being one of the most powerful nations on earth, is one of the most literate nations in world history.

Generation after generation of immigrants who came to this country immediately recognized the significance of obtaining an education in order to participate in America's economic and social opportunities. To them, public education was America's welcoming gift, an endowment that offered them a shot at a better life. It enabled the nation's newest residents, or at least their children, to pursue the American dream. Unfortunately, as the years passed and the children of those immigrants assimilated into the fabric of American society, appreciation for public education began to fade.

By the 1960s, education had all but evaporated from the public's radar screen, and chagrined educators strove desperately to get education into the consciousness of the general public. National polls never showed education to be in the nation's top ten priorities, and very few national politicians ever mentioned education in their stump speeches.

Education reform was rarely discussed because education was rarely discussed. The status of public education and the plight of America's teachers were not on anyone's agenda, and teachers knew it all too painfully.

America's public schools had long been staffed with dedicated, professional teachers who worked hard year after year to produce a literate and knowledgeable citizenry. They still are. Teachers have always taken their education mission seriously, and they deeply care about the young people they teach. Amazingly, however, in spite of the incalculable contribution teachers have historically made to American democracy, and in spite of their positive effect on the lives of millions of future citizens, their contribution continues to be greatly undervalued. It is more than safe to say that during the last two hundred years the teachers of America have become its buried treasure. There are unquestionably many reasons for this unfortunate situation, but here are a few.

Mandatory education for all children eventually morphed from a privilege to an entitlement. Over the last century, and particularly since World War I, a free public school education has come to be viewed as part of the routine of American living. To put it another way, because all children are now obligated to attend school, over the generations what parents once viewed as an *opportunity* has been ratcheted down to an *obligation*. Notwithstanding this shift in perception, educating all America's citizens in order to make them productive members of society is more important now than ever.

Teachers are held responsible for providing a quality education to every student even though they are not responsible for what happens to those students when they aren't in school. It is an indisputable fact that poor children come to school for the first time lagging behind children who are not poor, a handicap that follows many of them throughout their lives. Often, poor children don't have a home environment conducive to learning, and some children endure home lives so frightful that their efforts at school, as well as their attitudes about life, are seriously impaired.

Teachers try desperately to reach students who have trouble learning. The stories they tell about their students are gut wrenching: kids who sleep in a different home (or place) virtually every night; kids who watch their parents or caretakers do drugs; kids who make some progress while in the nurturing environment of the classroom only to slide backward when they return to a corrosive home situation; kids who have no role models except the drug pushers, gang bangers, and pimps who populate their neighborhoods; kids who are frightened to walk back and forth to school; kids whose parents both work; and kids whose most nutritious, and perhaps only, meal of the day is provided at school.

Some students have very few people in their lives who really care about them or spend time with them, and one of those people is often a teacher. In light of all this, it's especially tragic that preschool programs in many states are being cut back at the very time they should be expanding, and teachers are constantly being asked to do more with less. It's no less appalling that millions of this country's students have no health insurance protection whatsoever. For a nation as prosperous as America, it's scandalous that we don't do more to guarantee every youngster a safe environment, enough food to eat, and adequate medical care.

Society has overlooked the teaching profession because women have dominated its ranks. In America, sad to say, professions that have been largely populated by women, like teaching and nursing, have been relegated to a less favorable status than professions dominated by men. Theoretically, that shouldn't be the case, but it is, especially where the rubber hits the road: pay and prestige. This deplorable situation is no coincidence and is discussed later in the book.

Public schools are funded, and teachers are paid, directly from public tax dollars. Because public schools are funded almost exclusively through public tax dollars, they fall prey to the fashionable sport of criticizing anything related to taxation. To a degree, that's understandable; few people want their taxes increased, and most would like them lowered. Unfortunately, the all-too-prevalent, knee-jerk opposition to any school tax increase, no matter how much it is needed, often means reduced school budgets, and reduced school budgets usually mean a reduced quality of education. Public school accomplishments are often marginalized by antigovernment, anti-taxation, pro-privatization rhetoric. A good example is the way some people label public schools "government schools" with the full intention of making it a pejorative term.

The antitax phenomenon is an increasingly ruthless problem for schools, and the large number of Americans who no longer have children in school makes the problem severe. Only about 25 percent of the people living in any given community in America today have children attending public schools. In communities with a high percentage of retirees on fixed income, the situation is exacerbated even more. The public's disdain for increased taxes, when combined with taking the public schools for granted, is a devastating one-two punch to the solar plexus of American public education.

Tax cutting zeal turned to madness in the 1970s, and proved to be dreadfully harmful to children and education. The state of California led the way. For many years California legitimately touted one of the best education systems in America, but over the last twenty-five years its education system has fallen precipitously behind. California's collapse into an education sinkhole began with the passage of Proposition 13, a populist 1978 ballot initiative that dramatically rolled back taxes and gutted quality education in the state.

California still struggles with massive budget deficits and atrophied public services, and its education system has dropped like a stone from its former place of education preeminence. Ironically, tax cutting has caused Californians to harvest two bad crops: a substandard education program *and* a state in financial tumult.

Unfortunately, Proposition 13 kick-started a frenzy of tax rollbacks across the country, most of which adversely affected public education. These rollbacks, to one degree or another, decreased school budgets and caused savage cuts in many programs, including fine-arts and language education. It is ironic that the rollback juggernaut hit education at the very time that America needed more, not less, from its education system in order to compete in the emerging high-tech, global marketplace of the information age.

Teachers have been relegated, along with other government employees, to a kind of depressing, "public-servant" netherworld. This categorization is related to antigovernment, anti-tax sentiments. It lumps teachers into a cohort of so-called public servants—a dreadful term for public employees—that trivializes their professional standing. By condoning the "public servant" mindset generation after generation, society has given itself a justification for tolerating the poor pay and working conditions of its schoolteachers. They are, after all, government employees, and *servants* at that.

Public schools are accused of being riddled with incompetent teachers. This canard is both virulent and unjustified. Sure, there are some bad teachers in America's schools, just as there are bad practitioners in every profession and occupation in the world. Anyone who denies the existence of some incompetent practitioners within a cohort of over three million public school teachers is either a liar or a fool. Teacher unions have been reluctant to admit the existence of even *some* incompetent teachers for fear that education's critics will distort that acknowledgment to claim that *most* teachers fall into that category.

The relatively few bad teachers in the ranks disproportionately harm the reputations of the good and excellent ones, causing them to pay a high price in public perception and confidence. Finally, while I'm no media basher by any stretch, bad teachers make headlines; good ones don't.

There is a long-standing perception that just about anyone can teach school. Public education in America is a gargantuan enterprise, with more than 50 million young people occupying classrooms in more than fifteen thousand local school districts containing more than eighty-eight thousand schools. In many communities, the public school system is their largest employer, their largest transport system, and their largest food supplier. It takes well over 3 million teachers to educate those 50 million kids. Because teachers are so numerous and accessible in their communities, their existence and nurturance is just assumed, like trees growing in the park. After all, some believe, if there are so many teachers, how hard can teaching be?

The belief that teaching is a job that just about anyone can handle completely disregards what teachers do and how they do it, and displays a lack of knowledge about the challenges and difficulties of being a teacher. Every day, teachers face the complexities of educating a roomful of thirty or more squirming, energetic, inquisitive students with the attention span of a firefly. Maintaining student discipline while at the same time establishing and maintaining rapport with them is difficult enough in and of itself. Actually getting students to ingest and digest the subject matter takes knowledge, patience, understanding, and a big dollop of magic.

While doing all that, teachers must contend with virtually every aspect of society's problems and challenges, because they march through the door every day. To cite but one example, America is experiencing its largest immigration in history, and its impact on the public schools is colossal. In many American schools, students speak more than one hundred languages, and teachers figure out ways to reach them and educate them. It reminds me of the admonition that Ginger Rogers danced all the same steps as Fred Astaire, and had to do it *going backward*.

The absurd assumption that teaching is easy emanates in part from the fact that everyone who ever went to school considers himself or herself somewhat of an expert. Yet some of the brightest parents in the world can't figure out how to get through to their *own* kids. Sometimes, no matter how earnest parents are, and no matter how hard they try to convey their knowledge and experience to their progeny, they sometimes get back attitude, defiance, and disengagement (the triple torments from hell for any parent). Teachers do their thing in classrooms every day with those very kids and thirty or so others *just like them*.

CHAPTER 2

The Unprofession of Teaching

One of the great experiences of life is to make a positive difference in the lives of others. Teachers make that positive difference every day with the students they teach. Clear evidence of this fact is the number of people who unabashedly praise teachers who changed their lives, kindled an interest in learning, inspired a career path, solved a personal problem, opened a door, changed an attitude, or who just provided hope. In addition to the time they spend in the classroom, teachers, whether they practice in the Bronx, Bangor, or Boise, spend countless hours worrying about their students, preparing lesson plans, attending curriculum meetings, talking to parents, grading papers, doing administrative paperwork, administering standardized tests, and on and on. Most of all, they try to inspire kids to learn.

Christa McAuliffe, the astronaut-teacher from New Hampshire who was killed in the 1986 *Challenger* disaster, inspired untold thousands of youngsters to take an interest in science and flight because of her dedication, competence, and bravery. Before her death, Christa taught her students to dream, aim high, and work hard. She was a wonderful woman and an outstanding teacher, but hundreds of thousands of Christa McAuliffes in America's public schools never get the credit or publicity they deserve.

They teach and inspire their students without fanfare or recognition, and they often make personal sacrifices to do so. Many teachers, particularly in the elementary grades, routinely dip into their own pockets to purchase equipment, books, learning aids, and other items for their students. A recent article in the *Washington Post* reported that many elementary school teachers spend up to 10 percent of their already inadequate salaries to purchase supplemental teaching materials for the kids in their classes. Good teachers see any student's success as their own success, and any student's failure as their own failure.

If people could be flies on the wall in faculty lounges across the country, they would hear teachers chatting about how students responded to something they were teaching. They'd hear stories of ideas that worked and of those that flopped. Best of all, they'd hear teachers talk about "magic moments," those wonderful times when a youngster's face lights up as he or she suddenly "gets it." Teachers also like to talk about the illusive but profound "teachable moment" when an opportunity to learn presents itself and must be seized immediately or perhaps lost forever. For teachers, successfully taking advantage of those moments is like winning the educational lottery.

It doesn't take an Einstein to deduce that quality teachers are at the epicenter of a quality education. Unfortunately, attracting quality teachers into the profession is becoming more and more difficult. Many prospective teachers, particularly women and minorities, are taking jobs outside education that pay much more than teaching. It is commonplace today for twenty-year veteran teachers who are earning the maximum on their district's salary schedule to see their own children, fresh out of college, taking entry-level jobs with salaries that are double or triple their own. As pathetic as that situation is, it's even worse that American society tolerates it. No wonder there is a shortage of qualified teachers.

Some education pundits contend that the solution to the shortage of qualified teachers is to staff America's classrooms with former military officers, second-career homemakers, and retired mathematicians and scientists. In order to attract such people, these pundits call for the elimination of teaching certificates, teaching degrees, and college teacher-training courses. They propose instead to hire people who are "experts" in the subject matter, contending that if someone knows the subject matter, they can teach it. Such proposals are superficial at best and counterproductive at worst, and are a throwback to the popular assumption that anyone can teach school.

It's an unassailable fact that successful teaching requires knowledge of the subject matter. Of course it does. Teaching, however, does not always equate with learning. Many incompetent teachers have mastered the subject matter only to find themselves clueless about how to get the material across to students. Knowing the subject matter without being able to get through to students is like the old story about the dog food company that was going bankrupt even though it had the best factories, the best packaging, the best scientists, and the best ingredients in the dog-food business. After extensive research, they discovered the problem: dogs just didn't like the stuff.

Attracting excellent teachers to the profession is only half the solution. An even bigger issue is keeping good teachers in their classrooms after they've been hired. Research indicates that about 40 percent of the American teaching force leaves the profession within the first five years, and in urban areas the percentage is even higher. This alarming statistic reflects the irrefutable fact that what teachers face today in American classrooms is infinitely more difficult than what their predecessors faced just a generation or two ago. Poor working conditions, noncompetitive pay, bureaucratic red tape, and the preoccupation with high-stakes testing exacerbate the inherently difficult job of teaching, and more and more teachers burn out early in their careers.

Given the obstacle course that teachers constantly have to hurdle, crawl under, and crash through in order to remain in the classroom, it's a downright miracle that such a high percentage of excellent teachers remain in public education at all. Teachers are unjustifiably knocked all the time, and it's time to set the record straight. In my last address to the ten thousand delegates to the NEA Representative Assembly in Chicago in July 2000, I said the following:

> Over the years, I have gotten much more from NEA than I have ever given. It has been my honor to work for you. It has been both my vocation and my avocation. . . . But much more meaningful, and much more appreciated, than all the wonderful experiences that have filled my professional life are the things that have filled my heart. I have had the golden gift of working with the greatest staff that any organization has ever had. Their contribution to NEA is incalculable, their dedication and talent immeasurable, their commitment unrelenting. I have worked with terrific and courageous elected leaders over the years, people who have been a great source of inspiration to me and provided a thousand memorable experiences. Most of all, my inspiration has been the teachers of

America and the young people they teach every day. I've seen the steely look of determination in the eyes of teachers struggling to find that illusive, teachable moment for an uncomprehending student—and shared their sheer joy when that moment produced results. I have seen tears in the eyes of teachers totally frustrated by their lack of support from school districts, parents, and politicians. I have seen courage beyond description as school employees fought those who tried to push them under. I could literally take hours telling you stories of public school employees who risked their reputations, their jobs, and even their lives in order to advance educational, human, civil, union, and professional rights.

CHAPTER 3

Rudely Awakened

In the fall of 1955, I enrolled at Michigan State Normal College, a highly regarded teacher-training institution that became Eastern Michigan University (EMU) a few years later. I selected Eastern because it was located in Ypsilanti, a town fairly close to Detroit, and because I knew a student who went there. Unfortunately, I decided to dedicate my first year of college to higher living instead of higher education, a course of action that caused me to flunk out of school after my freshman year.

My departure was memorable. One Thursday afternoon at the conclusion of my freshman year, Dean "Bingo" Brown, EMU's venerable and highly regarded dean of men, sent me a letter inviting me to be in his office at 2:00 p.m. the following Tuesday. Dean Brown was in his eighties and had a reputation for being a tough old bird even though he looked and sounded like a geriatric version of television's Mr. Rogers. At the appointed time, I went to his office to make my case (the fact that I had absolutely no case to make didn't deter me in the slightest).

Just as almost everyone remembers exactly what he or she was doing on the day President Kennedy was assassinated, I remember my conversation with Dean Brown as vividly today as if the intervening half-century didn't exist. In fact, that conversation is engraved in my memory like a mental tattoo, word for word and syllable for syllable. As I entered his office, Dean Brown put me at ease right away by placing his hand on my shoulder and brandishing an incandescent smile.

Me, *looking serious and scholarly*: Good afternoon, Dean Brown. You sent for me?

Bingo, *the smile more avuncular*: Mr. Cameron, Mr. Cameron. It's very good to see you. I've been looking forward to this meeting. Please have a seat. Would you like some coffee?

Me, *sitting in the designated chair, apprehensive but confident*: No thank you, Dean Brown. I drank all the coffee I could stand while studying for my finals last week.

Bingo, *a tighter, bemused smile*: Mr. Cameron, do you mind if I call you Don?

Me, *ready for a stern lecture*: No sir, Dean Brown. Please do.

Bingo, *a faint smile, but a frown in his eyes*: Good. Good. Don, have you had a good time here at Normal?

Me, *throat constricting*: Yes sir, I've had a great time.

Bingo, *no smile, and his eyes had the look of a prison chaplain counseling a dead man walking*: I felt sure that was the case, Don, and I'm very happy for you. I really am. However, next year you won't be having your good time here at Normal. You'll be having it somewhere else. Drop me a line and let me know where that might be. I always like to hear from former students. Good luck and thanks for coming in. That'll be all.

And it was. Even though I was embarrassed to be out of school, I decided to cool my heels in Ypsilanti for two reasons. First, just weeks before flunking out, I had met and begun dating a beautiful EMU freshman student named Ida Jane Arcand. Even as young and stupid as I was, I knew immediately that she was special and that I needed her in my life on a permanent basis. We were married in August 1958.

The second reason I stayed in Ypsilanti was that I had a full-time job with United Airlines at Willow Run Airport. A month or so after being married, I decided it was time for me to get serious about an education, not to mention future employment, so I made an appointment to see Bingo Brown. After I explained to him that I had settled down with a terrific young lady (very true), come to my senses (somewhat true), and given up beer (a lie), he said, "OK, Don, I think you're ready to get an education. I'm letting you in, but don't let me down."

I didn't. I got my bachelor's and master's degrees within the next four years. Thirty years later, in 1985, Eastern Michigan University presented me with an Honorary Doctorate in Education, and in February 2001 I was honored beyond description to be admitted as a charter member of Eastern Michigan University's Education Hall of Fame.

Eastern Michigan, like most colleges, sponsored a job fair each spring, and school districts sent representatives onto the campus to interview potential teaching candidates. Teachers were in great demand, and finding a job wasn't very difficult for most of Eastern's graduates. Many were offered jobs in exotic-sounding places on the west coast, and friends signed teaching contracts in places like Redwood City, Pasadena, San Francisco, Anchorage, Fairbanks, and Portland. We were all bursting with enthusiasm, eager to begin teaching, and extremely naïve. I signed a contract in Birmingham, Michigan, a wealthy Detroit suburb.

It didn't take me long to get a real education about education. In most ways I was well prepared for the actual teaching part of the job, but I was almost totally unprepared for the palpable disregard for the opinions of teachers within the district and the marginal status of teachers within the community. It didn't take me long to discover that it wasn't only the teachers in Birmingham who felt the sting of second-class citizenship, but also teachers all over Michigan and around the country.

Negative or condescending attitudes toward teachers and teaching were old hat to veteran educators. The marginalization of teachers has a long and sordid history in America, much of it stemming from discrimination against women in the profession. Over the years, a male-dominated society had deemed teaching and nursing to be a safe, acceptable career path for women. Teaching school was viewed as a kind of babysitting, tutoring function for which females were well suited. Until World War II, many single female teachers had to sign contracts with their school districts that pledged them to refrain from dating, getting married, getting pregnant, or drinking.

In the earliest days of public education, a high school diploma was considered sufficient to become a teacher. Men who went into teaching entered a woman's profession and were therefore subject to its parameters, one of those parameters being low pay. Men were paid very little, and women were paid even less. Society's tightfistedness was abetted by the goofy, self-serving rationalization that teachers weren't motivated by income, but by altruism—as if the two were mutually exclusive. A corollary rationalization was that, while teaching didn't pay much, those who became teachers went into the profession with their eyes wide open.

Yet another justification for low salaries was that women teachers provided a second income for their husbands, and since the husband was the family breadwinner, a female teacher's pay was really just butter for the bread. When education associations petitioned school boards for additional teacher pay, the breadwinner argument was repeatedly trotted out as the reason for not raising salaries or providing fringe benefits of any kind (75 percent of the faculty were women). Well into the 1960s, that rationale was used to ensure that teachers had no medical care or other fringe benefits provided by their employers.

In most school districts across America, there were no paid health-insurance benefits, no paid dental insurance, no life insurance, and no 401(k) type supplemental retirement plans. Nothing. Nada. Bupkes. Most states had modest retirement plans for teachers, but it was clear that after thirty or forty years of teaching they would retire at or below the poverty level. School boards and superintendents often explained that teacher pay wasn't really that bad if you considered family income.

Such shallow attitudes were distressing, demeaning, and acidic to the morale of teachers. It was particularly depressing because, in addition to all the teaching and related assignments, I often worked late into the night and weekends correcting papers, preparing lesson plans, gathering materials, and doing administrative paperwork. My colleagues and I asked ourselves repeatedly why we were working so hard, doing a good job at something so important, only to be undermined by disapproving attitudes and condescension.

During my four years in the classroom, my friends and I would often compare notes about how members of the community made derogatory comments about teachers. In social settings, for example, if someone declared that they were an architect, or a lawyer, or a real estate agent, or a dentist, or an insurance representative, or a stockbroker, the conversation simply went on. But, if a teacher revealed what he or she did for a living, people often felt compelled to make a snide remark that ran the gamut from indifference, to insult, to pity. Teachers felt much like the character Cellophane in the musical *Chicago*: taken for granted and used.

At a parent-teacher meeting one evening during my first year of teaching, the father of one of my students shook my hand and told me how appreciative he was of the job I was doing. He and his wife told me that at dinner almost every evening their son reported enthusiastically about what I had been teaching that day. Then the father said something that still rings in my ears almost forty years later: "Mr. Cameron, most people who go into teaching aren't smart enough to get into a real profession, but my wife and I think you're an exception." He might as well have hit me between the eyes with a mackerel. I was shocked, deeply offended, and—worst of all—clueless as to how to respond without being furious. He meant his insensitive remark as a compliment, but it was an awful thing to say, particularly to a teacher.

A year or so later, after I had acquired my sea legs and developed a little more self-confidence, I bumped into the same guy at a community event and invited him to have a cup of coffee with me. I told him how much I had enjoyed teaching his son, but said that after all this time I was still troubled by the remark that he'd made to me at the parent-teacher conference a year earlier. I told him I just couldn't believe he actually meant what he had said because the vast majority of teachers I knew were well-read, intelligent, and energetic people who could have been successful in virtually any field they chose.

I also told him that Birmingham and other Michigan school districts were very fortunate to have teachers of such high intellectual caliber in their schools, particularly given the low salaries being paid. I considered my remarks illuminating if not persuasive. He looked at me like I had just coughed a hairball into his coffee cup, and replied, "I remember very well what I said, Mr. Cameron, but I was only saying what everyone knows. It's a fact of life. Listen, if you want to do something for yourself, get out of teaching and get a real job."

Attitudes like that dampened the idealism of way too many enthusiastic teachers in Birmingham and around the country. Worse, it made them jaded. Every teacher we knew, with relatively few exceptions, worked hard and took their jobs to heart. They strove to be creative and responsible with their students, trying to be professional. However, neither society in general, nor the education establishment in particular, really gave a damn—not in 1862 and not in 1962. Teachers silently ingested this kind of disrespect year after year, generation after generation, and it rankled.

Disrespect for teachers was no less the case within the education community itself, although it surfaced in very different ways than within the public at large. School districts, as well as state departments of education and state legislatures, wanted no part of teacher participation in education decision making. Consequently, with very few exceptions, *teachers had no role* in deciding what salaries they were paid, what curriculum they taught, where they were assigned, how long they worked, what working-environment conditions prevailed, what textbooks they used, what teaching methods they employed, or what policies governed their professional work. When teachers reported for their teaching assignment, they were handed a set of school-district policies and a course of study for their subject area, and then they were monitored to make sure they did exactly what they were told to do.

An occasional enlightened school superintendent or visionary building principal would seek teacher input and try to establish a team atmosphere, but those individuals were relatively rare. Once in a while, a local school district would form a committee of teachers and administrators to discuss textbook selection or curricula, but teachers were reluctant to serve on those committees because their recommendations were almost always ignored. It was made clear to teachers that education decisions were the unilateral domain of the local administration and school board.

Teachers were continually admonished to be professional, but they had none of the characteristics of other professions: they lacked any ability to make independent professional judgments, they had virtually no influence over their own salaries, and they exercised practically no control over the policies of their profession. Even worse, their opinions, individually and collectively, were neither sought nor valued; they simply weren't part of the education power structure. For America's teachers, professionalism was largely a shallow euphemism for indentured servitude. What happened in Birmingham was being replicated in district after district around the state and around the country, and many, many districts were demonstrably worse. The pot was boiling.

CHAPTER 4

The Factoryizing of Education

It's more than ironic that in the 1960s, when collective-bargaining statutes finally made teachers decision-making partners with school boards regarding their wages, hours, and working conditions, school boards and administrators fulminated that collective bargaining created an adversarial, labor-management atmosphere. They contended that collective bargaining would destroy the "education family" that had always existed between school boards, administrators, and teachers. Nothing could have been more revisionist.

It's certainly true that collective bargaining acknowledges an adversarial relationship between labor and management as part of the process. Conveniently overlooked by the revisionists, however, was the fact that a rigid labor-management structure within public education had been in full force and effect since the industrial revolution. That industrial model, cloned directly from the private sector, had been superimposed over public education and the teaching profession for over a century, and that model dealt school boards and administrators all the high cards.

Margaret Haley, a union leader for both the National Education Association (NEA) and the American Federation of Teachers (AFT) in the early 1900s, called the overlay of corporate structure on public schools the "factoryizing of education." The industrial model imposed a top-down management straightjacket on public education that dominated the relationships between school boards, administrators, teachers, and even students. Haley proclaimed that the system made teachers little more than "automatons whose duty it is to carry out mechanically and unquestioningly the ideas and orders of those clothed with the authority of position." Haley was absolutely on target way back then, and that system was still in full force fifty years later when collective bargaining for public employees finally came along.

The industrial model organized public schools like corporations. The school board was the board of directors that set corporate policies, the superintendent was the CEO who ran the show within those policies, the central-office administrators were the company executives, and the building principals were the middle managers who relayed directions to the workers. Teachers, just like assembly-line workers, were at the bottom of the labor-management food chain. As Haley said, their job was to implement unquestioningly the decisions of the board and management.

Teacher input was viewed as irrelevant to the school board (the corporation) because teachers (the line workers) were hired to do as they were told and leave managing and decision making to others. Just as an automobile assembly-line worker was not expected to know about designing cars or making the assembly line more productive, teachers were not expected to know about designing curricula or making their classrooms more productive. School boards and administrators literally "teacher proofed" both school curricula and teaching methodologies so that teachers couldn't influence predetermined educational policies and procedures. Teacher judgment and creativity were shoved into the janitor closet.

Notwithstanding the industrial model's death grip on public education, the teacher revolution of the 1960s could easily have been avoided if school boards, legislatures, and the public had simply been willing to recognize teachers as true professionals and treat them accordingly. To do that, of course, would have meant paying them a professional salary, treating them with professional respect, and giving them a seat at the decision-making table. A full century after the industrial revolution, when it became abundantly clear to teachers that *nothing* was going to change for them, the teacher revolution became inevitable.

Moreover, the industrial model didn't hamstring professional educators only; it also affected public school students. The system valued rote learning and classroom discipline as the hallmarks of a good education, and deviation from those norms was forbidden. Even as late as 1960, most school districts forbade teachers to arrange their students' desks in a configuration other than straight rows facing the front of the room. Teachers who tried to create cooperative-learning environments by having students move around in the classroom or talk to each other in work groups were criticized as lacking classroom discipline.

The emphasis was on orderliness, not learning. Al Shanker, AFT president until his death in 1997, told about feeling besieged and needy when he first entered the classroom in New York City in the 1950s. He felt encouraged when the school principal appeared in his doorway and stood there for several minutes. Anticipating a suggestion or two from the principal about what he had observed, the principal said, "Mr. Shanker, there is paper on the floor over on the third aisle." Then he walked away. Shanker's experience was typical. Nonconforming teachers were at high risk of receiving negative evaluations by their principals regardless of what learning was actually taking place.

The industrial superstructure also dramatically affected students' academic and employment future. It was accepted that about 15 percent of the students in American schools would go to college and get jobs that required them to make decisions (managers). It was also accepted that roughly 85 percent of the students would go on to occupy relatively high-wage, low-skill jobs as members of the industrial work force (line workers). The industrial/educational mindset, which worshipped efficiency, determined that it would be inefficient for society to pay for a quality, academically oriented education for the lower 85 percent of the students who were headed for the labor force. Consequently, they were relegated to high school industrial-arts classes or perhaps a trade school.

Clearly, America accepted the idea that its priority was to provide a quality education only for those students who would become managers or professionals (doctors, lawyers, politicians, architects, financiers, etc.) One glaring manifestation of that philosophy was the "tracking" system instituted in most public and private schools. Kids were evaluated early on as to which category they fit (laborers or managers), and then were herded into their respective academic corrals, called tracks. Of course they weren't publicly called labor and management tracks; they were labeled trade or college-prep paths.

You didn't have to be a rocket scientist to predict that tracking would disproportionately and adversely affect minorities, girls, and the underprivileged, which it did. Tracking lost favor during the civil-rights and women's movements of the 1960s and '70s, but it institutionalized a pattern for educating kids that still exists today. The problem with the old 85:15 ratio is that America today demands higher-order learning skills and literacy from virtually all its students. Business and industrial leaders are keenly aware of that reality. Yet America's education system is still basically attuned to the old 85:15 percent ratio.

The public schools of America provide a superior education by any standard, national or international, for the top 15 percent of the school population. The truth is, however, that federal, state, and local governments are not willing to spend the kind of money it will take to provide a quality education for the lower 85 percent of the student population—those who need the most attention.

In the 1980s, the business community recognized the need for high school graduates who could do a lot more than work on assembly lines or unload trucks. They needed workers who could think, reason, work in teams, run high-tech equipment, and make decisions. The old industrial system of education wasn't producing the kind of high school graduates needed to be competitive in a global economy. That impetus from the business community, combined with the *Nation at Risk* report caused the focus on education reform and the subsequent flogging of public education to begin in earnest. The problem is that expecting an education system rooted in the industrial age to produce for the information age is like whipping a twenty-year-old horse running in the Kentucky Derby, and blaming teachers astride an antiquated system is like blaming the jockey astride an old nag.

CHAPTER 5

The Anvil of Democracy

In America, the idea of educating all its citizens is one of the key components of our democratic form of government. More than ever, it is patently obvious that public education is profoundly important to both the fulfillment of American democracy and to the nation's survival. In the cauldron of modern global politics and economics, an educated citizenry is not a luxury; it's a necessity. To put it another way, the importance of education to America's way of life—and its future—is undeniable. Thomas Jefferson, one of the more perceptive founders, said it eloquently: "Education is the anvil upon which democracy is forged."

Democracy without an educated citizenry is a contradiction in terms, and the linkage between democracy and education is of profound importance. Exactly because America's health, economic growth, and cultural success depend on an educated populace, every American should understand the fundamental role that education plays in our society. American democracy is a real tribute to the vision and insightfulness of the country's founders. They created a nation with a radically different governance structure, a government literally "of the people, by the people, and for the people."

While those words are still inspirational more than two and a quarter centuries after their origin, words alone, however inspirational, cannot sustain any government. A democratic government is dependent upon the very people it serves, and those people are obligated to run it, nurture it, and—most importantly—understand it.

When America's founders molded their new government, they weren't just politicians spouting rhetoric and striking heroic poses.

They were literally under the gun, functioning in a politically charged atmosphere that posed grave personal consequences for all of them. Keenly aware that their words and actions could lead to war with England, they knew their necks were literally on the line. When Benjamin Franklin uttered the immortal words, "We must all hang together or we will surely all hang separately," he wasn't kidding. These guys were, after all, promoting revolution against their government.

In that context, the words "of the people, by the people, and for the people," memorialized in the Declaration of Independence, were not only bold, but also dangerously provocative. Nevertheless, the founders pushed forward, sublimating their own fears for the good of their fledgling nation. When deliberations about the new government took place in the Continental Congress and later in the Constitutional Convention, the debates often ran hot, sometimes to the boiling point, and the new government more than once teetered on the brink of collapse.

When the hubbub subsided, virtually all the founders had agreed on a simple but profound principle: If the new democracy was to survive and thrive, if it was to sustain itself long beyond their lifetimes, *an educated citizenry had to be its cornerstone*. They not only committed themselves to be participants in their own government, they committed the *future* citizens of America to be its stewards. They left us a heavy responsibility.

Even though their definition of citizenship differed from ours today, the idea of educating a country's citizens flew in the face of all other governmental systems in the world. Those governments were exclusively some form of monarchy, theocracy, or dictatorship, all of which held their citizens largely uneducated and powerless. Europe, after all, was not far removed from its feudal history. Our founders were determined not to create a nation controlled by corrupt kings, religious potentates, military despots, or even an all-powerful president. Rather, they sought a nation where the citizens were responsible for their government and the government was accountable to the citizens. All of this was, indeed, revolutionary stuff.

However, while the idea of an educated citizenry was incredibly avant-garde, a definitive system for how to educate Americans was not established at the onset. The Constitution is silent on which level of our system (federal, state, or local) should be responsible for educating its citizenry. That's not surprising, since the idea of public schools, per se, did not advance until many years after the Constitution was adopted. The current system of school authority and responsibility, including funding, has evolved over the years through a combination of policy, consensus, and tradition—much like voting rights and political parties.

Public education, even though financially starved throughout the years, has provided an education for countless Americans: farm kids, city kids, rich kids, poor kids, and immigrant kids, not to mention all manner of adults. In spite of both its unspecified beginning and chronic underfunding, public education has managed to produce a literate society and world leadership in virtually every field of human endeavor. Nonetheless, a revamping of how public education is funded today is sorely needed.

Specifically, the federal government should accept the primary responsibility for providing the financial resources necessary to ensure a quality education for all Americans, especially those at the bottom of the economic ladder. Funding a much larger share of public school costs does not mean federal control of education. State and local communities should still manage public education, but fully funding school budgets has become almost unbearable for most of them. Most states spend between 35 and 40 percent of their budgets on education, and they have to fund all the other social demands placed upon them. Their plight is compounded by the fact that many states have a constitutional prohibition against deficit spending, which the federal government, obviously, does not.

Currently, only about 6 percent of public education funding comes from the national level, while about 94 percent of school funding comes from state and local resources. America is one of a very few industrialized nations that decentralizes school funding to such an extreme. In the developed nations of the world, on average about 54 percent of the funding for elementary and secondary schools comes from their central governments. The government in this country should provide at least 60 percent of the cost of public education. Some conservatives will blanch at that suggestion, but it is an idea whose time has come.

If we were to establish a public school system from scratch today, hardly anyone would advocate the fragmented and illogical school-funding scheme that has evolved over the years. Our nation's founders certainly wouldn't have. Securing a quality work force for quality American jobs, especially in a changing economy, is a national imperative. It's obvious that providing a quality education for all American students is the key to our economic, social, and military future. It only stands to reason, therefore, that education should be treated as a national mission and priority.

CHAPTER 6

Can't Get No Respect!

In many respects, I was fortunate to begin my teaching career in Birmingham, an academically progressive school district that sought to be on the cutting edge of new curricula. I was crazy about teaching—that is, crazy about the time I spent with students individually and in class. However, much of the rest of being a teacher just made me crazy. Birmingham had all the trappings of an affluent suburban school district: wealth, new buildings, a superb faculty, competent administrators, and a school board focused on education. Unfortunately, in its genuine pursuit of educational excellence, it also condoned a subculture that advanced all the traditionally negative frustrations teachers lived with: low pay, no fringe benefits, arduous working conditions, patronization, and lack of participation in education decision making.

The Birmingham School District rowed hard when it came to quality curricula and enhancing its academic reputation, but when it came to teacher salaries and working conditions, it was more than content to rest on its oars. My teaching colleagues were terrific, and we tried mightily to contend with the burdensome layers of responsibility that were piled on top of actual classroom work. There were dances to chaperone, after-school clubs to proctor, faculty meetings, football and basketball games that we were encouraged to attend and sometimes work, homecoming events to plan and patrol, various charity drives, parent-teacher nights, Parent Teacher Association (PTA) meetings, hallway patrol, lunchroom duty, bus duty, and on and on. School faculty meetings, held with mind-numbing regularity, were almost always boring, unproductive, and irrelevant affairs. I've often said that when I die I want to die in a faculty meeting, because the transition between life and death would be so subtle that I'd never know the difference.

It didn't take long for me to discover that teachers in schools all over the state were grumbling about their salaries and working conditions, and the grumbling wasn't confined to the state of Michigan by any stretch. In talking to other teachers at various state and national meetings, I heard firsthand how gnawing economic problems plagued teachers from Maine to California, eroding their morale and shortchanging their families. Teaching was a profession for those with a Mother Theresa complex. To put it in the vernacular, teacher pay sucked.

Teacher economic depravation in the 1960s was simply an extension of what had always existed. Pay for teachers in America had been a chronic disgrace since the inception of public education. In 1857, the year the National Education Association (NEA) was founded, most teachers worked in one-room schoolhouses and were paid less than a hundred dollars a year. The great American educator, Horace Mann, addressed the pay issue when he spoke to the delegates attending NEA's second annual convention in 1858: "Our first duty as educators is to do the best we possibly can to educate the nation's youth. Our second duty is to obtain salaries commensurate with our first duty." Over a hundred years later, the first duty was being accomplished, but the second one never left the gate.

In the 1800s, teachers often received no salary at all, as many local communities paid their teachers by providing food or lodging. The conditions under which they taught school were appalling, with teachers laboring all day in stuffy, one-room schoolhouses that accommodated children of all ages and grades. In addition to teaching, they were expected to clean the schoolhouse, maintain the fire in winter, and exhibit a personal life of almost puritanical rectitude. As indicated earlier, single women teachers were especially vulnerable. If a married female teacher became pregnant, she had to resign her teaching post as soon as the pregnancy showed. If she didn't resign, she was summarily fired. If, God forbid, an *unmarried* teacher became pregnant, she was not only summarily fired but also publicly humiliated.

Since women teachers were viewed as economically subservient to men, they were paid less than men were. Their status as second-income earners gave school boards all the rationale they needed to refuse to provide them with decent salaries. Both women and men teachers bristled at the system's blatant sexism, but bristling and complaining got them nowhere; they and their teacher associations had no power, no authority, and no leverage. What they did have was burgeoning anger.

As the industrial revolution moved along, high school diplomas, or even two years of college, were no longer considered adequate training to become a teacher. By the time World War I ended, teachers were expected to be proficient in the subject matter and to have three or four years of college—maybe even a degree. The upgrade in teacher education resulted in a more professional approach to teaching, and school districts were forced to offer teachers actual salaries—not much, of course, but salaries nonetheless.

As the industrial revolution spawned corporate bureaucracies, those structures became the model for public education. The resulting top-down management systems in education served to institutionalize pay inequities, encourage sex discrimination, and minimize teacher input. The pattern of treating teachers as low-level employees, not professionals, didn't change over the next one hundred years.

In the South, black teachers in segregated schools earned about one-third of what their white counterparts earned, and all southern teachers, black and white, earned considerably less than their counterparts in the North. They still do. In addition to paying women less than men, school districts routinely paid elementary teachers less than secondary teachers. The funding of schools increasingly depended on taxes, mostly local property taxes. Of course education was underfunded as a result, and, any way it was sliced, teachers came out with the short end of the economic stick.

Since NEA's inception in 1857, professional associations provided little practical help in improving teacher pay. Edgar B. Wesley, the author of *NEA: The First Hundred Years; The Building of the Teaching Profession*, wrote that for the first fifty years of its existence NEA focused on things other than salaries:

> While the NEA passed various resolutions calling for higher salaries, for more than half a century it did little to secure them. The educational leaders assumed that the building of a profession took precedence over problems of the personal welfare of teachers; that once the profession

was established, teachers would naturally achieve status, security, and dignity.

Unfortunately, NEA's "meek shall inherit the earth" approach produced catastrophic results for its teacher members. Focusing on the profession and professionalism brought virtually no improvement in salaries and working conditions. What *did* happen was that America got more and more comfortable paying teachers poorly, and teachers got less and less comfortable being poorly paid. The pressure was building.

A contributing factor to increased teacher militancy was the return to the workforce of thousands of veterans from World War II and the Korean War. During this period, the public-employee sector of the American workforce expanded greatly, and a significant number of veterans who attended college under the GI Bill entered the teaching profession. The percentage of males in the teaching profession increased from 20 percent in 1940 to over 30 percent in 1960. Those new male teachers were broadsided by the harsh economics and pseudoprofessionalism they found in teaching.

For the most part, these newcomers were not second-income wage earners, and the economic realities of teaching became very problematic for them, especially if they had families to support. While most Americans were reaping the beneficence of a hot postwar economy, teacher pay was worse than ever. After the war, teachers in some local communities became angry enough to strike over the raging inflation that followed the price controls of wartime. Local strikes took place in Norwalk, Connecticut; Buffalo, New York; and St. Paul, Minnesota. NEA neither instigated nor approved of these job actions. In fact, NEA did not change its policies to support teacher strikes until the 1960s.

Those early strikes were a harbinger of things to come, because the abysmal pay afforded teachers was metastasizing. It had gotten to the point where school boards saw absolutely no need to significantly increase teacher salaries, *even when they could clearly afford to do so*. Teachers were paid on the basis of supply and demand: school boards could *supply* whatever salaries they wanted, and teachers could *demand* nothing. The criteria used by every school board to determine salaries for its teachers was to compare itself with what surrounding school districts were paying. If one school district paid its beginning teachers $5,000 per year, for example, its neighbors tried to stay within $50 to $100 of that figure.

Because school boards had all the power and teachers had none, and because superintendents informally coordinated teacher-pay levels from district to district, that arrangement smacked of being a monopoly. When coupled with the parsimony of local taxpayers, this approach effectively restrained both property taxes and teacher salaries.

In the 1950s, a new salary construction for teachers, the single-salary schedule, began to take hold. This device, which is still utilized in virtually every school district in the country, was designed to eliminate the most obvious and arbitrary abuses of teacher pay. The single-salary schedule pays the same salary to all teachers who meet two criteria: years of experience and college degrees or credits earned. With the advent of this pay system, teachers were guaranteed a minimal pay increase for every year's experience on the job, and they could earn more if they completed an advanced degree or acquired other specified academic credits. If nothing else, it eliminated arbitrary, uneven, and subjective payments to teachers.

As teacher pay languished, other professionals were earning considerably more money. According to the 1960 census figures and NEA research, here's how the average annual pay for professionals stacked up around the time I began teaching:

Doctors	$19,794
Lawyers	$16,082
Architects	$8,779
Accountants	$8,541
Teachers	$5,264

In most school districts, it took teachers twenty years to double their income on the salary schedule. If they started at $5,000, for example, twenty years later they might make $10,000. Twenty years! Even worse, if teachers moved to another school district, they most often received little or no experience credit for teaching in their previous job— in other words, they had to start at the beginning of the salary schedule all over again.

Many families simply could not afford to live on a teacher's income. Either both spouses worked, or the teacher worked two or three jobs, or both. During my four years of teaching, I worked as a sales clerk in a Montgomery Ward department store, and I also supervised recreational basketball for Birmingham students on weekends. While at Derby Junior High, the principal offered me the opportunity to coach the Derby intramural football and track teams, and I jumped at the chance to earn a few extra dollars. No matter how hard I worked, our family always slipped further and further behind.

Even finding the time to work additional jobs was difficult because of the many hours teachers were required to work, which went far beyond actual classroom time. To add insult to injury, in order to move up the salary schedule, teachers had to earn more college credits and advanced degrees. They paid for the coursework out of their own pockets and took them largely during the summer when they were "on vacation." Almost every teacher I knew preferred to teach a full year and be paid accordingly, but that option wasn't available. By the 1960s, the drums of rebellion were beating louder and louder.

Over forty years later, the working conditions and salaries of American teachers have improved in relative terms. Their improved professional and economic status, however, did not happen because politicians experienced a revelation, or because school boards had an epiphany, or because a concerned general public demanded it. Teachers are better off today because they organized, joined unions, and embraced collective bargaining. That's the truth.

CHAPTER 7

Tenure Anyone?

Low pay and bad working conditions weren't the only problem facing teachers and their organizations. Their job security was tenuous at best, and an abomination at worst. School boards and superintendents were free to hire and fire whomever they wished, whenever they wished, and for whatever reason they wished. For example, from the 1930s through the 1950s, it was a fairly common practice for districts to fire more highly paid, experienced teachers in order to hire newer, inexperienced teachers with lower salaries.

One of the most egregious practices of all was the firing of some teachers in order to make room for friends and relatives of the superintendent or school-board members. All too often, teachers who disagreed too strongly with a school administrator were fired on the spot. Athletic coaches were routinely promoted to administrative posts, including that of superintendent, and minority teachers were rarely hired into white districts. Teacher criticism of the system was not tolerated, and those who did so placed their job squarely on the line.

Rumblings against deplorable hiring and firing practices had begun during the 1920s and intensified partly because of protestations from NEA and AFT. In 1942, Kate Frank, an Oklahoma teacher activist, was fired from her job without warning and without any kind of hearing because she had organized an effort to unseat several school-board members in an election in a school district where she lived but did not teach. When she decided to fight her dismissal, NEA took her case to court on the grounds that her right to free speech had been violated.

Frank's case led to NEA's establishing a permanent legal defense fund in her name to protect other teachers who were victims of arbitrary dismissals. She won her case and was reinstated to her job in 1945. Tenure laws began to be enacted by legislatures in state after state to protect good, experienced teachers from political abuse. Tenure laws simply mandate that fired employees must have the charges against them spelled out, may confront their accusers, and can request a hearing before the school board. They also have the right to appeal the board's decision to the state tenure board, which has final authority.

For many years, until collective-bargaining contracts came into existence in the 1960s, tenure laws were the only protection that individual teachers had from arbitrary dismissals. Currently only three states—Georgia, Mississippi, and Texas—have not enacted laws to protect experienced teachers from arbitrary dismissal.

Tenure laws were never designed to protect incompetent teachers, and the popular notion that tenure laws make it impossible to fire incompetent teachers is largely bogus. Without question, some incompetent teachers over the last sixty years have benefited from these laws, but untold numbers of incompetent teachers *have* been fired. On the other hand, tenure has saved hundreds of thousands of perfectly competent teachers from wrongful dismissals. Tenure laws afford teachers a fair dismissal process—nothing more, nothing less.

Incompetent teachers should never benefit from tenure, but there are two primary reasons incompetent teachers occasionally slip through the due-process net. First, school districts sometimes fail to adopt clear teacher-evaluation policies and can't document a teacher's incompetence. Second, and more common, districts have adequate teacher-evaluation policies but *don't follow them*. All too often, school principals initiate dismissal proceedings against a tenured teacher without a shred of documented evidence to support the dismissal: no classroom observations, no written evaluations, no records of parental complaints, nor any other type of proof. It is, in fact, fairly common for teachers being fired for incompetence to have nothing but glowing evaluations in their files from school administrators.

Teacher unions have sometimes gone overboard in using procedural technicalities to prevent obviously incompetent teachers from being dismissed. What is often overlooked, however, is that unions have a legal obligation to protect the rights of members being disciplined or dismissed by a school board. If teachers who are being fired feel the union isn't representing them sufficiently, they can, and do, sue it claiming a lack of "fair representation."

A good teacher union will encourage school districts to consider remedial action before dismissal to see if the teacher's shortcomings can be corrected. Unions also successfully work in partnership with school boards and school administrators to counsel obviously incompetent teachers out of the classroom. It happens every day. There is, of course, no public record of those collaborative efforts because school administrators are not prone to publicly credit teacher unions, and teacher unions are not prone to publicize their role in getting rid of incompetent teachers.

Bad teachers who engage in criminal behavior, such as sexual misconduct with students, providing them with drugs or alcohol, and so on, should *never* be in *any* classroom. Tenure laws should never be used to shield illegal behavior, and teachers found guilty of illegal activities involving students should be prohibited from teaching anywhere. All too frequently a teacher is hired and then later discovered to have a criminal past. Such occurrences not only mock the hiring process, but they endanger students. School districts, particularly large urban districts that are constantly under the gun to recruit large numbers of teachers, must have sound screening and hiring practices.

CHAPTER 8

A Century of Tea and Crumpets

Before collective-bargaining statutes gave teachers some degree of collective power, most teachers joined their local, state, or national education associations because it was the "professional" thing to do. Of course, they also joined because school administrators, particularly building principals, recruited them. In my case, the principal at Derby Junior High in Birmingham personally welcomed me to the school and handed me an association membership form. He said that he was sure I'd want to join the association because he was very proud of the Derby faculty's 100 percent membership in the Birmingham Education Association (BEA). Here I was, a brand new teacher brimming with enthusiasm and optimism, being personally told by my building principal how proud he was of his school's BEA membership record. I was inspired to join.

My recruitment scenario was replicated hundreds of thousands of times in schools throughout the country. In addition to joining their local associations, teachers were encouraged to join the state and national associations as well. Unification, the NEA policy that requires members to join all three levels of the association when they join their local, did not come into effect until 1972. Prior to that, membership in the national organization was optional. When I signed up, the local Birmingham dues were two dollars, the state dues five dollars, and the national dues ten dollars. I considered that a lot of money.

Prior to collective bargaining, the Birmingham Education Association, the Michigan Education Association (MEA), and the National Education Association were "tea-and-crumpets" professional organizations. The same was true of virtually every other state and local teacher association in the country. In Birmingham, like everywhere else, the local association board of directors was comprised of members elected from the various school buildings throughout the district, and many of those BEA building reps were school principals. There was also a local executive committee of seven members, three of whom were school principals. Association membership encompassed the entire education "family," but associations had very little power, and what power they did have was rarely used.

BEA's programs and activities ranged from discussions of curricula to discussions of district policy, to discussions of state legislative actions, to discussions of MEA and NEA activities, to discussions of national and international education issues, to discussions of social events, to discussions of what should be discussed next. BEA discussions of district policies or curricula almost invariably took place *after* the school board or superintendent had already made the decisions and announced them. BEA did ask the superintendent each year for salary increases, but there was no formal process and certainly no assurance that the board would give the proposal consideration—or even see it.

Most often, if a teacher was unfairly disciplined or dismissed, BEA would petition the building principal or superintendent on that member's behalf. In such circumstances, however, it was always clear that *petition* was the operative word. To a teacher in trouble, association representation meant little more than moral support. Having a local association leader plead the member's case was occasionally successful, but only when it was clearly proven that the school board had violated its own personnel policies or the state tenure law.

It was a difficult situation for local associations because they represented the professional interests of both the teacher in trouble *and* the administrator bringing the charges, both of whom were likely to be association members. As a result, associations had to balance advocacy for teacher members on the one hand with advocacy for school administrators on the other. Because there was no union, no collective bargaining, and no negotiated master contract, conflicts between the interests of teachers and administrators could be demonstrably ridiculous.

To cite one example, in a pre-collective-bargaining school district in Iowa in the 1960s, the school board unilaterally gave the teaching staff a paltry raise. At an all-membership meeting, the president of the local association recommended that the association reject the increase. The school superintendent, a voting member of the local association, spoke against the recommendation. After the debate concluded, the teachers, by a voice vote, resoundingly agreed to reject the increase.

When the president declared the result, the superintendent took the microphone and announced that he considered the vote too close to call. He asked all those who had voted against the board's offer to stand on the right side of the room, and all those who supported it to stand on the left. The vote suddenly became overwhelmingly in favor of accepting the board's offer. That kind of occurrence was common; school boards and superintendents constantly admonished teachers to be professional, but rarely treated them as if they were. Such was the state of things around the country during the pre-collective-bargaining years. Teacher associations were virtually powerless to improve the lot of their members, whose frustrations continued to mount.

At the national level, NEA enjoyed a prestigious and cozy relationship with both the education establishment and the federal government. In fact, the Department of Health, Education and Welfare, as well as state departments of education, relied heavily on NEA's research division to provide accurate data about public education in America. Similarly, most large NEA state affiliates provided those services for their respective state governments.

The national organization had been a star in the establishment firmament for generations. NEA had been incorporated and chartered by an act of Congress in 1906, with President Theodore Roosevelt signing the charter on June 30 of that year. As a result of its efforts to improve public education—including its involvement in such endeavors as the creation of the modern American high school, international education, the establishment of the United Nations Educational, Scientific, and Cultural Organization (UNESCO)—NEA had garnered a prestigious reputation in education and political circles. Ironically, while NEA wielded enough clout to influence public education policies generally, it carried comparatively little weight when it came to improving the salaries and working conditions of its teacher members.

Even more ironically, with school superintendents and other high-ranking administrators dominating the organization, NEA and its state affiliates were part of the very power structure that kept teachers'

salaries and working conditions depressed. NEA's advocacy for increases in teacher pay was largely rhetorical and consisted mostly of
passing resolutions, establishing goals, and producing research reports.
By 1957, NEA was the largest publisher of educational material in the
United States. NEA's approach to higher salaries for teachers was predicated on the lunacy that improving education and printing comparative
teacher salaries would somehow inspire school boards, legislatures, or
the tooth fairy to do right by America's teachers.

While NEA was doing its education thing, it adamantly opposed
unionizing its members and collective bargaining, viewing such activities as "unprofessional." Neither did NEA support teachers' getting involved in electoral politics. NEA did not support candidates for public
office because the specter of teachers being labeled unprofessional
prompted the organization to muzzle itself. Consequently, NEA didn't
endorse its first candidate for president of the United States until 1976,
when it went for Jimmy Carter.

Voluntary abstinence from the political process effectively discarded
another potential tool that teachers could have used to improve their lot.
Without collective bargaining, without political action, and without a
strong organization, there wasn't much hope for real improvement in
the lives of the association's members. Even local associations that
brandished a more militant stripe on their sleeves found it exceedingly
difficult to exert much leverage on school boards when the only
weapons available to them were comparative salary data and prolonged
whining.   .

In other words, while the organization pontificated about low pay
and bad working conditions for teachers, it rejected any practical way
to do anything about them—especially if it meant bucking the establishment. NEA and its state affiliates did lobby Congress and state legislatures for increases in school funding, but even when additional
funds for education were forthcoming, the money rarely went directly
to teacher salaries.

Teacher strikes were not much of an option either. Strikes by local
NEA affiliates were exceedingly rare because the affiliates not only had
to confront school boards, but also opposition from their own state and
national associations. Their professional associations saw those activities as—you guessed it—unprofessional. NEA didn't remove its poli-

cies against striking until the 1960s, and only then because members forced it upon them.

As late as 1966, Dr. William Carr, NEA's longtime executive secretary, railed against teacher strikes, urging members to abide by the ethics of the profession and not "be goaded by indifferent or hostile public officials to act in ways that create an unfavorable image in the public mind." He also said, "It is my considered personal opinion and advice that the use of strikes by the teaching profession for the economic advantage of the teacher will impair, and ultimately destroy, the confidence of the public in the teacher."

Several years later, as teachers at the local association level began to press for collective bargaining, Carr implored NEA affiliates and leaders to seek state "professional negotiations" legislation that would include school administrators within the bargaining units. He urged, "militant teachers must get into the trenches with militant superintendents and principals so they could fight for the same purposes." Such esoteric proclamations were impractical, abstruse, and raw meat for the young lions of collective bargaining in local associations all over the country. They knew that Dr. Carr and his minions were living in a fantasy world, a world that kept teachers subjugated and poor.

CHAPTER 9

The Hundred-Dollar Mistake

NEA's transition from professional association to union came rapidly in the mid 1960s—almost overnight. Like a rubber band stretched beyond its limitations, the revolution was inevitable given the long history of societal abuse and association paternalism heaped upon teachers. The revolution began in the only meaningful place it could possibly succeed—among the rank and file. In spite of the fact that the rapid changeover was traumatic for many association members, they surged forward nonetheless.

An impatient membership was not about to wait another century for NEA to wise up. They had waited as long as they were going to wait. They discarded the threadbare, hand-me-down cloak of *professionalism at all costs*, and determined to be more demanding (i.e., militant) in order to improve their own lives, as well as the lives of the students they taught. Collective bargaining provided NEA members, through their organizations, a chance for legal parity with school boards, and they weren't about to be deterred. This parity led directly to a degree of association power that, in turn, led directly to improvements in the lives of school-board employees.

The story of what happened to my colleagues and me in my local school district of Birmingham, Michigan in 1964 and 1965 is more than instructive because it exemplifies what was happening, one way or another, in thousands of districts across the country. Over the years, I have talked to the vast majority of leaders from that period, and their stories, still remarkably vivid, contain astounding degrees of uniformity. The common denominators in these stories are low pay, terrible working conditions, school-district arrogance (or insensitivity), and public indifference. These commonalities bolstered teachers' determination to stand up and fight against continuing the status quo.

My first teaching job was at Derby Junior High School in Birmingham, Michigan in 1962, where, with a master's degree, I was paid a salary of $5,300 a year. I became active in the 1,100-member Birmingham Education Association from the beginning, and during my second year the Derby faculty elected me as one of its BEA building representatives. That same year, 1963–64, the school board unilaterally raised every teacher's salary $100 for the year, the equivalent of $8.33 per month. In deciding on that amount of money, the board didn't examine the district's ability to pay, didn't consider for a nanosecond whether or not teachers could live on their existing salaries, and certainly didn't ask BEA for its opinion or recommendations. The board, upon the recommendation of the superintendent, simply looked at salary schedules in surrounding districts and put up enough money to stay even with them.

Low pay and miniscule annual salary increases had long been a burr under the saddle of Birmingham teachers. At the behest of a large number of BEA members who were upset with the paltry $100 raise, the association formed a special salary committee to look into the district's finances and push for a much higher salary increase for the following year. As members of the committee, we felt strongly that the board should do three things regarding Birmingham teachers' salaries: solicit input from the teacher association before making salary decisions, become aware of the degree to which teachers considered the $100 raise totally inadequate, and provide a substantially larger raise for the following year.

The BEA membership admonished the committee to pull out the stops. Consequently, we analyzed the district's current and past budgets; compared Birmingham's salary schedule with those of similar school districts throughout the country; determined what teachers were making compared to other professions and occupations; and even calculated the estimated savings that the board would incur the following year because of employee turnover (higher-paid teachers leaving and being replaced by newer, cheaper ones).

We discovered that over the years the board had built up a budget surplus of several million dollars—more than enough money to give every teacher a significantly hefty salary increase without negatively impacting the district. After much debate within the committee, the majority voted down those of us pushing for a salary increase of at least $500 because they didn't want to appear greedy (I still can't believe how brainwashed we were). The committee agreed to request a $300 salary increase for the following year. BEA requested a meeting before the school board to make its presentation. The request was granted and a date set.

Being true to our nature as teachers, the committee had augmented its presentation with charts, graphs, a variety of tables, and a recapitulation of the most salient points. The grand finale of the presentation was the recommendation for the $300 salary increase for the following year. We had, of course, emphasized during the presentation the board's ample ability to pay based on its multimillion-dollar budget surplus. When we finished, the president of the school board smiled and said, "Thank you very much for that outstanding presentation. You certainly did your homework. It's obvious that Birmingham deserves its reputation for employing excellent teachers. The school board will adjourn for a short period, and then we'll come back and give you our response."

They couldn't have been gone ten minutes before reentering the room. The board president cheerfully pronounced,

> Let me say again on behalf of the board how much we appreciated and enjoyed your presentation. Needless to say, we believe you deserve much more than a $300 raise, and we'd like nothing better than to give it to you. Unfortunately, while it is true that the district has a rather large surplus, the board feels it is only prudent to save those funds for a rainy day. Consequently, we've decided to give the teachers another $100 salary increase for next year. Thanks very much for being here tonight and thanks again for all your hard work.

Before leaving, we asked what the board meant by "saving the surplus for a rainy day." The board's response was a rapid succession of inanities: they viewed the surplus as a reserve fund; they had to prepare for the possibility of an emergency (undefined); and they were practicing good, conservative budget management. My colleagues and I were more than angry, and our anger rose in inverse proportion to our sinking morale. What had us so riled wasn't just the summary rejection of our proposal; or the almost abusive, in-your-face $100 raise; or even the futility of having worked so hard for months only to run into a brick wall.

What rankled most was the board's utter disregard for the economic situation of our families even while acknowledging the district's ability to pay substantially more. Birmingham teachers were living at or below the poverty level while the school board boastfully squirreled away millions of dollars for a vague, theoretical rainy day. As one of the committee members said, "They patted our heads, picked out pockets, and kicked our asses all in one motion."

The members of the board were not evil people, and I personally liked several of them, but their patronizing attitude toward the teaching staff was maddening—and degrading. As frustrating as that experience was, the board simply did what boards had been doing for a century. Low teacher pay had become so institutionalized that boards actually felt comfortable keeping it that way; they were simply doing their job.

For the 1965–66 school year, I was elected president of the Birmingham local. As fate would have it, that was the same year the Michigan state legislature passed the collective-bargaining law for public employees, including teachers (P.A. 379). Immediately after the enactment of the statute, Birmingham teachers, along with teachers in hundreds of other Michigan school districts, went to the bargaining table for the first time to negotiate with their respective school boards. As BEA president, I chaired the negotiating team even though I knew absolutely nothing about negotiating a contract—none of us did. Fortunately for us all, BEA received a great deal of assistance from the Michigan Education Association, the same organization that had opposed the legislation only a few months earlier.

In a visionary and practical move, MEA cooperated with NEA to provide several experienced labor attorneys from a prestigious New York City law firm (Kaye Scholer LLP) to help certain MEA locals bargain their first contracts. The idea was that if select Michigan local associations could do well in their first round of bargaining, it would serve as a beacon for others to follow in the years ahead.

Much to my delight, Birmingham was picked as one of the lighthouse districts, and an affable bear of a man named Seymore "Sy" Goldstein soon appeared at BEA's doorstep. He was one of the firm's lawyers, and he immediately became a mentor and advisor to the BEA negotiating team. Another attorney from the firm assigned to Michigan that year (Saginaw and Midland districts) was Bob Chanin, who went on to play a major role in the collective-bargaining arena as NEA general counsel.

Birmingham was a good choice for selection as a lighthouse district. It was a typical suburban school district with a good reputation and a progressive approach to curricula. The teachers in Birmingham were also typical of teachers throughout the state. Like their counterparts, they were paid poorly and were involved in a variety of extracurricular activities, often without remuneration. They loved teaching kids, but most of them were struggling mightily to make ends meet.

When collective bargaining became suddenly available, Birmingham teachers didn't engage in philosophical discussions about whether or not it was "professional." They wanted it. Likewise, there was very little hand-wringing over the issue of separating from school administrators in order to form a bargaining unit. On the other hand, they knew exactly what they *did* want: higher salaries, better working conditions, and enough legal power to make their professional lives better. They clearly viewed collective bargaining and unionism as the vehicle for their economic and social deliverance.

Even after embracing collective bargaining and unionism, however, teachers within the NEA environment were very sensitive about being viewed by the pubic as members of a traditional labor union. The transition from professional association to union was psychologically traumatic for some members in the collective-bargaining states, and because of this sensitivity, conventional union nomenclature was softened, while euphemisms abounded.

For years, collective bargaining was referred to as "professional negotiations" within NEA circles. That term worked for two reasons: first, NEA had been using the term for several years to describe its own version of a collective-bargaining statute, one that included school administrators within the bargaining units; second, to many members, the term *professional negotiations* seemed less associated with trade unionism. Similarly, we didn't negotiate "contracts"; we negotiated "master agreements." Strikes were not "strikes"; they were "walkouts," "job actions," or "professional leave days."

Such euphemisms were pretty silly, but most of us recognized that it would take a little time for some teachers to make the adjustment to more traditional collective-bargaining language. Union labeling never bothered me because I was born and raised in the union ghetto of Detroit, and my relatives and friends all belonged to unions. Anyway, like many others, I was just eager to get going and didn't care what things were called.

Consequently, my choice of words sometimes got me in minor difficulty with my Birmingham colleagues. For example, in one of the newsletters to the membership during the first round of bargaining, I reported that we told the board's negotiating team that we needed much higher salaries in order to put food on the table, but the board offered us nothing but peanuts. The next day, I received at least a dozen calls from members telling me that I shouldn't use such confrontational language because it sounded too unionlike.

On another occasion, the local newspaper, the *Birmingham Eccentric*, printed a story about the bargaining situation and said something to the effect that the Birmingham Board of Education was negotiating with the teacher union. Three or four days later, I received a petition from over 250 association members demanding that I get the *Eccentric* to apologize for calling BEA a union. Embarrassed to do so, I nonetheless made a call to the editor and asked him to refer to BEA as a professional association. I got no apology, no retraction, and no sympathy. What I did get was about fifteen seconds of laughter, during which time he paused only long enough to say to someone, "Hey Fred, get on the line and listen to this." When the next edition of the *Eccentric* came out, we were still a union, but I was relieved that the paper didn't report my phone call.

Because of the BEA membership's determination to achieve significant results at the negotiating table, while at the same time having an aversion to union identification, I worried about whether the teachers would stand tall when the chips were down. I soon found out. During a particularly frustrating negotiating session, the board's team accused the BEA team of presenting the demands of only a few strong-headed leaders, not the entire faculty. They said they didn't believe that their employees would be so demanding.

Consequently, we asked the membership to attend an upcoming school-board meeting to show their support for the BEA negotiating team. Members were urged to attend the board meeting en masse to let the board know clearly that the constituents supported their team and that they were, in fact, responsible for the demands being made at the table. Ironically, the leaders' biggest problem had been tamping down the expectations of the membership when it came to demands placed on the bargaining table.

We had surveyed the entire teaching faculty in writing, asking for their input and suggestions. In addition, we met with the faculties of every individual school building in the district to discuss the survey results. The overwhelming majority of the BEA membership made it crystal clear that they wanted certain immediate reforms or improvements in the contract: a significant salary increase of *at least* 15 percent; increased supplemental pay for mandatory extracurricular requirements (some of which paid nothing at all); class size reduction; a duty-free lunch period; board-paid health insurance (there was none); increased sick-leave days; and a shorter mandatory work day (teachers had had to report for work an hour before the kids did in the morning and stay an hour after they left in the afternoon).

As the time for the school-board meeting approached, there was much apprehension about how many members would show up. Although our demands accurately represented the members' wishes, I worried about whether the teachers would do something as public as take part in a demonstration, especially one where the school-board members, superintendent, and central-office administrators could see exactly who was present. When the appointed time arrived, about 800 of the 1,100 BEA members appeared at the demonstration.

Many of the participants were very nervous when they left their homes, but were reassured to see so many of their colleagues at the administration building. The demonstrators were pumped up, and without any direction from anyone they decided to form two single-file lines all the way from the back parking lot to the front entrance of the building so that school-board members, the superintendent, and the central-office administrators would have to walk right through the corridor of teachers as they walked from their cars to enter the front door of the building. Many teachers talked to school-board members as they went by, assuring them that the BEA negotiating team did, in fact, represent them and their issues.

By any standard, the evening was a huge success. If nothing else, the board and its negotiating team stopped claiming that the BEA team did not represent the membership. During the demonstration, however, something happened that for me epitomized the teachers' schizophrenia about their union status. A group of teachers from one of the elementary schools had decided to make picket signs and bring them to the rally. The signs said things like, "We Support our Team," "Negotiate in Good Faith," "We Don't Want Another $100 Raise," "You Sit on a Surplus While We Sit on the Poverty Line," and that sort of thing.

They rolled up to the demonstration in a pickup truck containing about a hundred of the signs loaded in the back. Teachers eagerly took the signs and were more than happy to hold them where school-board members could see them, but they would not carry them while walking. In a mystifying way that only they understood, holding the signs to demonstrate support was OK, even holding them in front of the board members was OK, but picketing—even informational picketing— smacked of private-sector unionism. Their collective reasoning may have been as simple as not wanting members of the community to see them picketing, or it may have resonated from somewhere much, much deeper in their professional psyche. Go figure. That event marked the first time that the school board and superintendent began to see the dual role that teachers would occupy in the future: employees of the school district *and* union members.

After several months of negotiations during the winter of 1965 and the spring and summer of 1966, including four or five all-night sessions just prior to the scheduled opening of school in September 1966, we reached agreement with the board on a three-year contract. The salary schedule for the first year of the agreement guaranteed an average salary increase of $975 per teacher, plus the regular step increments, which averaged another $200. That meant that virtually every member of the Birmingham Education Association would get a raise of at least $1,175. In addition, the school board agreed to pay part of our hospitalization insurance, a major breakthrough.

We also negotiated other provisions into the contract that made our professional lives better. For one thing, every teacher was guaranteed a duty-free lunch period of thirty minutes. For another, teachers were no longer mandated to attend PTA meetings on their own time. Every provision within the master agreement was settled for the next three years except the school calendar and the salary schedules for the second and third years, which were to be negotiated in each of those years.

There is little doubt that without collective bargaining and a more militant approach by teachers and their unions, Birmingham teachers today would still be eating with their students during a twenty-minute lunch period, they would still be required to spend hours and hours of their own time and money attending noninstructional school and community events, and they would still have to work two or three jobs to make ends meet. So would teachers in every other district. In my speech to the 2000 NEA Representative Assembly in Chicago referenced earlier, I talked about the age-old dilemma of professionalism and unionism:

> There is a cacophony of conservative voices today claiming that unionism and professionalism are in opposition to each other. Nothing could be further from the truth. For us, professionalism without unionism is an empty vessel, and unionism without professionalism is no less empty. I know this to be true from my personal experience. Before NEA was a union, it was strictly a professional association. It spent its time thinking professional thoughts and doing professional things. NEA was held in the highest esteem by America's education and political establishment, and NEA was literally awash in the glow of professionalism. However, beneath that professional veneer, beneath the lofty language, beneath the glow, teachers were being systematically patronized and povertized. Sophie Tucker once said, "I've been rich and I've been poor. Rich is better." Folks, I've been a professional without a union and a professional with a union. Union is better. I believed that in 1965, and I believe it no less today.

After the first round of bargaining in Michigan, many large urban and suburban local associations decided to hire a full-time staff person to handle negotiations and related matters. Within a two- or three-year period, about fifteen of these local staffers emerged, including me in Birmingham. In order to employ a full-time executive director—and receive a subsidy from MEA and NEA—a local association had to open an office and hire both an executive director and an office secretary.

Michigan's local staffing program was subsequently merged into NEA's Uniserv (United Services) program, which employed a professional staff person at the local level for every 1,200 NEA members. These staffing programs accurately reflected the rapid growth of collective bargaining and membership in the NEA affiliates. Many of the local staffers later went on to become executive directors of NEA state affiliates around the country, NEA staff members, or both.

As more and more local associations engaged in collective bargaining, new and unprecedented internal issues arose. One of the more emotional issues to rear its head was that of teachers who refused to join the union but still received the benefits of the union's bargaining efforts, including salary and fringe-benefit increases. Not only did nonmembers receive the benefits of the union's salary increases, they also pocketed the cost of union dues that everyone else had to pay. The situation occurred because public-employee bargaining laws mandate that union bargaining representatives must bargain equal benefits *for all members of the bargaining unit*, not just for those who are union members. This statutory inequity quickly became a source of great irritation to association members, and they sought to eradicate the disparity by negotiating *agency-shop* provisions into their master contracts.

Simply stated, an agency-shop provision obligates nonmembers of the bargaining unit to pay a fee to the union that is somewhat equivalent to the union's costs of bargaining and administering the collective-bargaining agreement. Agency-shop provisions are perfectly legal and have a long tradition in union collective-bargaining contracts. Members felt strongly that if people who do not pay union dues benefit equally from the bargaining efforts of the union, they should at least have an obligation to help support the cost of that bargaining. They see agency shop as principled and just. However, this concept drives some right-wing, antiunion groups nuts, and they get their knickers in a bunch over the notion that someone is forced to pay a fee to a union they don't want to join.

Anyone who doesn't want to join a union, for whatever reason, shouldn't be forced to. Yet, any way you cut it, nonmembers are free riders. They get something for nothing and leave the heavy lifting to those paying the dues and doing the work. In BEA's first year of bargaining, for example, the efforts of the union produced at least $1,000 more per teacher than the traditional $100 salary increase provided by the district. Look at it this way: if someone decided not to pay taxes for police and fire protection while still receiving the same protection as tax payers, how fair would that be? Would the government stand for it? Would the taxpayers?

The three-year contract that had been mutually agreed to by the school board and the BEA during the first round of bargaining included a substantial "no-strike" clause prohibiting the association from striking for the duration of the contract. Why not such a clause, we reasoned. After all, the board had pledged to negotiate the second- and third-year salary schedules with BEA in good faith. The school board, however, had another plan in mind.

The board took the position that it had done very well indeed with faculty salary increases during the contract's first year (1966–67), and there was no need to improve salaries for the remaining two years beyond a little tinkering here and there. After months of absolutely fruitless talks between the parties, the BEA negotiating team became more and more frustrated. and the membership became increasingly agitated. The teachers felt that the first-year salary increases represented a good first step, but only a first step. They saw the board's foot dragging in the second round as a deliberate return to previous pecuniary insensitivity. They also felt that the board was determined to take a pound of flesh for the previous year's salary increases, and was deliberately thumbing its nose at them.

As the summer unfolded and Labor Day approached with virtually no progress, the teachers became furious. During several meetings over the summer, the membership told the negotiating team to relay their dissatisfaction to the school board. We did, but to no avail. On the eve of Labor Day, just prior to the scheduled opening of school, we held a meeting of all 1,100 members to report to them exactly where things stood and to solicit their feedback. We told them that the school board's "last and final" offer was a $25 across-the-board salary increase. While we anticipated strong support for a strike, we were determined that the members should understand exactly what they would be biting off if they did strike. Not only did state law prohibit public-employee strikes, but striking in the middle of a three-year contract containing a no-strike clause would engender a huge legal crisis. In addition, we had no idea how the community would respond.

We repeatedly made these points to the teachers, hoping that reason and fear would combine to hold strike action in abeyance, at least temporarily. The meeting was stormy and contentious as various members argued their point of view, sometimes passionately and harshly, but almost always articulately. It soon became clear that there was widespread sentiment among the rank-and-file members to strike. The BEA president, John Dunlop, addressed the irate members and told them unambiguously what they didn't want to hear: that a strike would not only be patently illegal, but would place all of them and the association in great peril. He told them that if they struck, they had to be ready to face the consequences. He got nowhere.

Somewhere toward the end of the meeting, the crowd shouted for me to give my opinion about whether or not to strike. Having seen that two hours of pulling on the reins had not worked, I replied, "Let's hit the bricks," to thunderous acclaim. Dunlop of course voiced his approval and joined in the exhilaration. Thirty-six years later, John still gives me a bad time, as well he should, about how I got the applause while he took the heat. He'll get over it some day.

Toward the end of the meeting, it was decided that a strike vote would be taken, by secret ballot, at an all-membership meeting scheduled for 7:00 A.M. the first day of school two days hence. Since all faculty, administrators, and school-board members were already scheduled to meet for the opening day of school at Groves High School at 9:00 A.M., we decided to meet at that same site at 7:00 A.M. In addition to its convenience, a positive strike vote would send a clear message to the superintendent, administrators, and school-board members.

At the BEA strike-vote meeting, which every member of the bargaining unit attended, the facts were laid out once more, the membership meeting of two nights earlier was recapitulated, and a brief discussion was held. There wasn't much need for prolonged debate because the membership had thoroughly discussed the issues and a possible strike at the Labor Day–eve meeting. Everyone was up to speed. The only real dissent expressed at the meeting came from a few of the football coaches, who pleaded that a strike would be harmful to their players' athletic futures. One of the football coaches made the classic mistake (a mistake made over and over again by other coaches throughout the country during similar strike meetings) of stating to the assemblage that he would vote against a strike "because I care too much about the kids."

That statement was immediately translated by just about everyone to mean that the football coaches didn't want to have a losing season by having to forfeit a game or two. The coaches' plea had the same effect as lowering a dead goat into a river of hungry piranha. Hundreds of noncoaching elementary and secondary teachers, especially the women, were outraged at the implication that they cared less about the kids than did the coaches and their "damned football season." I took secret delight in seeing the coaches get their comeuppance because they were the same guys who had pestered me endlessly throughout the months of negotiations, admonishing the team to hang tough, saying, "don't hesitate to tell them we'll strike."

After the debate, a secret-ballot vote was taken, and the membership overwhelmingly voted to strike (82 percent in favor). At exactly the same moment that the school-board members, superintendent, and school administrators entered the building to convene the annual back-to-school meeting, over a thousand Birmingham teachers walked right past them going in the opposite direction. The strike was on, and during its two-week duration only seven or eight of the eleven hundred BEA members entered the school buildings to report for work.

Obviously, the most vehement push for the strike didn't come from the coaching ranks; but, surprisingly, neither did it come from male secondary-school teachers. The real anger and push came from the women. It soon became apparent all across Michigan that it was the proverbial "little old ladies in tennis shoes" who led the charge and walked picket lines with courage and determination. They were fed up with being patronized and taken for granted even more than the male teachers were. It was almost as if they were striking for all their teaching sisters who had endured the humiliations of the power structure for over 150 years.

Only one short year after 250 Birmingham teachers had signed a petition to get the local newspaper to stop referring to BEA as a union, they enthusiastically went out on strike. However, the desire of teachers to be seen as professionals while embracing unionism has been consistent from the earliest days of bargaining in the 1960s. NEA membership surveys over the next forty years confirm without exception that the vast majority of NEA members, including those in Michigan, want to be members of a "professional association that bargains for its members." In other words, they don't want to sacrifice one for the other.

In any event, the 1967 Birmingham strike lasted two weeks and was acrimonious. Negotiations went nowhere as both sides dug in their heels. Toward the end of the strike's second week, the Birmingham Board of Education went to the Oakland County Circuit Court to seek a restraining order to prevent the strike from continuing. Dunlop and I were specifically named in the suit, along with the Birmingham Education Association and the Michigan Education Association. On Friday, September 15, 1967, we were ordered to appear in front of Judge William John Beer for the Circuit Court for Oakland County, Michigan.

The judge looked like he had been sent over from central casting. He was a fifty-eight-year-old conservative judge with a mane of white hair that contrasted dramatically with his flowing black robes. On the appointed day, hundreds of teachers packed the courtroom as he addressed them in stentorian tones. He ordered the Birmingham teachers to report to work the following Monday, and he made it abundantly clear that if they didn't obey his order he would throw the book at them. He added that John and I would go to jail "for a long time." Then, with swelling rectitude, he said, "I have something further to say, and I make it part of this opinion: The teachers of the Birmingham School District made a contract with the children of Birmingham, the school children who are in your professional charge; and you cannot . . . be allowed to depart from your obligation." We were then dismissed.

At a subsequent membership meeting over the weekend, the members decided to return to work the following Monday as ordered by the judge. The vote to return was not overwhelming, as a large bloc argued to defy the court order. BEA members had guts, and they were willing to send John and me to prison to prove it. After returning to their classrooms, most teachers were angrier than ever and voted to "work to the rule," which meant that they fulfilled their classroom teaching assignments, but refused to perform any extracurricular work not specified in the contract. After months of consternation and acrimony, the two teams finally agreed on a modestly improved salary schedule for the second year of the contract. The pressure eased, but the resentment continued.

As far as the Michigan Education Association was concerned, a judge's ordering BEA members back to work was not all bad. MEA had been extremely nervous since before the strike began; its attorneys were apoplectic about the illegality of BEA striking in the middle of a three-year contract. MEA did everything short of physically restraining us from walking out. There were many weeks when MEA's organizational sphincter was extremely tight, but once the strike began MEA helped in every way it could. The kind of aggressive, "devil-take-the-hindmost" attitude exemplified by the local Birmingham association leaders and members was by no means unique in Michigan or the country.

In 1968–69, the third and final year of the infamous three-year Birmingham contract, the teachers were still angry, and the board was still determined to keep salary increases to a minimum. After months of negotiations, the two teams reached agreement on the third-year salary schedule. The bargaining team and I felt strongly that the board had offered enough on the schedule to wrap up the third year.

The settlement wasn't terrific, but it was good enough to buy peace for a year and allow wounds to heal before negotiations on a successor contract were to commence. When the salary agreement was presented to the membership, it was rejected. Many members felt it wasn't good enough, others were still seeking retribution for having been forced back to school by the judge, and still others just needed to vent their spleen.

After the rejection, a new bargaining team was formed (with me still on it), and we went back to the bargaining table. To say further progress was grueling would be an understatement. The board contended that it had gone as far as it was willing to go, and rejection of the earlier tentative agreement was BEA's problem, not theirs. School began after Labor Day with no new agreement on the third-year salary schedule, and things within the BEA membership became ugly.

A relatively large faction of the membership wanted to reconsider and accept the settlement that had been rejected earlier, or at least something like it. Others just wanted the consternation to end for a while. A third group, however, wanted to strike again. While in the minority, they were very acrimonious and shrill. They disrupted meetings, demanded to strike for the second time within the three-year contract, and generally hurled invectives at the BEA leadership. This was a prime example of teacher militancy during that period coming from the bottom up instead of from the organizational top down.

I was somewhat stung by this group's criticism of the BEA leaders and felt it was unjustified (I suppose all leaders being criticized feel the same way). However, it was their kamikaze mentality that really bothered me. I felt that it would have been disastrous if this group held sway and Birmingham teachers went on strike again during the contract. Consequently, I repeatedly and pointedly told them so. Another, lesser consideration for BEA and MEA leaders was that another strike in Birmingham, coupled with other strikes taking place throughout Michigan, could cause the state legislature to consider more punitive measures against teacher strikes—or even to repeal the statute.

During long hours of introspection and discussion with other BEA leaders, I believed more than ever that those advocating a second strike were wrongheaded and shortsighted. Nevertheless, it was clear to me that I was becoming a lightning rod for much of the frustration being expressed by the vocal minority. I had two choices: either go along with the strike group (this time believing them wrong) or quit. I talked the situation over with Ida, and we agreed that it was time for me to step down as BEA's executive director.

Although I didn't feel depressed or abused, I did feel my leadership in that situation had outlived its viability. In late September 1969, I informed the BEA executive committee and board that I was resigning. I left BEA with no hard feelings, no regrets, and no job. One thing was for sure; I didn't want to leave the arena of teacher advocacy. It was a cause that coursed irreversibly through my veins. One door had closed, but another was about to open.

CHAPTER 10

The Michigan Education Association

Within a few days of my resignation, I received a telephone call from George Brown, director of communications for the Michigan Education Association, who asked me if I had another job. I said that I didn't, and he responded, "Good. Don't do anything. I have an opening on my staff for a field PR person to work with MEA locals. I'd like you to come work for MEA and me—right away."

By this time, Ida and I had two children: a daughter, Amanda, who had been born during my first year of teaching in Birmingham, and a son, Benjamin, who came along in 1967, the year of the Birmingham teacher strike. In September 1969, we moved to East Lansing, where MEA's headquarters was located, to begin the communications job I held with MEA for six years until I became the director of communications in 1975.

My new MEA job was taxing and multifaceted, and required considerable traveling around the state. It was, however, not nearly as stressful as my job in Birmingham had been. The other MEA communications staffer with whom I worked was Harry Boyes, a former radio announcer for WJR radio in Detroit. Because of Harry's many talents and contacts, he was perfect for the job of representing MEA to the Michigan media. George, Harry, and I made a solid team.

As a member of the MEA field communications staff, my plate was always full. Most of my time was taken up either working on local representation elections between MEA and AFT, or handling community relations for local associations experiencing collective-bargaining difficulties. In addition to working with locals, I was deeply involved in two statewide petition campaigns to prevent public-tax vouchers from being used to fund religious schools. Led by the Catholic Church, the effort in Michigan to fund religious schools from public funds was called "Parochiad."

I went to work for MEA at a critical and propitious time. During the early years of collective bargaining, MEA resolutely preached that the object of negotiations was to reach agreement on a contract, and 95 percent of the time that's what happened. Nevertheless, for several years in Michigan after passage of the statute, the number of teacher strikes escalated. In 1966, the first year under the collective-bargaining statute, Michigan had only nine teacher strikes, but in 1967, the year Birmingham struck, there were thirty-six, and by 1969 when I went to work for MEA there were up to sixty strikes a year. By any definition, that was a lot of strikes, especially considering that in the previous twenty years there had been less than 110 teacher strikes in the *entire country.*

Notwithstanding the number of Michigan strikes, every year hundreds and hundreds of Michigan school districts and local associations successfully completed contract negotiations without them. Even when strikes occurred, most of them were settled without much problem. Occasionally a strike could turn ugly if a local school board tried to unilaterally impose a contract on the teachers, or if they fired all the striking teachers and replaced them with scabs. When that happened, bitterness and recriminations often prevailed.

Those seeking someone or something to blame for the sudden spike in teacher militancy during the 1960s often lashed out at teacher unions (they still do). In doing so, however, they almost always blithely ignore the obvious: teachers were simply fed up with the hypocrisy and empty rhetoric of those who had power over them. They finally rose up against the double standard by which society expected them to be competent, caring, sensitive, intelligent, and educated guardians of their children's future while refusing to pay them a living wage.

In the 1960s, the opportunity for teachers to acquire at least a modicum of economic justice was at hand, and teachers weren't going to let that opportunity slip away. Because of its successes at the bargaining table—especially its willingness to strike to achieve its goals—MEA was in the vanguard of the collective-bargaining movement within NEA. In fact, Michigan rode the point for other emerging collective-bargaining state affiliates. Michigan was not by any means the only state pushing the collective-bargaining envelope, but MEA rapidly developed a large cohort of young, experienced staff and elected leadership.

A prime example was MEA's hiring of Terry Herndon as its executive director in 1969. Herndon, a dynamic and aggressive teacher negotiator from the Detroit suburb of Warren, became the youngest state executive director in the country, having assumed the Michigan job on his thirtieth birthday. He was not only unique because of his age, but also because he was a state-association executive director with a collective-bargaining (union) attitude.

Local affiliates in Michigan considered the assistance they received from MEA in those days to be extremely important. The assistance was especially appreciated because MEA had originally opposed the passage of PA 379 so vehemently. MEA's rivals, the American Federation of Teachers (AFT) and the American Federation of Labor–Congress of Industrial Organizations (AFL-CIO), had strongly supported the bill's passage. However, when the legislation was enacted and signed into law by Republican Governor George Romney, MEA unhesitatingly embraced the new statute. This about-face resulted from a hardheaded analysis of the situation by MEA's longtime executive director, E. Dale Kennedy, a former school superintendent.

Kennedy, along with some of his attorneys and staff, realized that MEA faced an organizational crisis of Promethean consequences. The decision to implement the new law aggressively became the keystone for Michigan's future—and NEA's. Irwin Ellman, a feisty, intellectual Detroit labor attorney hired by MEA, told Kennedy, "Look. You people don't have to worry about this statute if you don't want to. You can disregard it. There's nothing in the act that requires you do to anything. You can sit on the sidelines and quietly preside over your own liquidation as an organization."

Ellman was right on target, and Kennedy accepted his advice. If MEA had ignored the new legislation or, even worse, fought against collective bargaining, the results could have been disastrous. Especially given his background as a school superintendent, Kennedy's decision was both wise and pivotal; he knew full well that collective bargaining would let the genie out of the bottle.

E. Dale Kennedy's collective-bargaining epiphany helped push MEA and NEA to the front of the organizing parade. It was like Kennedy and Ellman stood at the edge of a cliff overlooking a raging river far, far below with only a few dangerous options before them. Then, like Butch Cassidy and the Sundance Kid, they leapt off the precipice into the torrent. They didn't know if they would survive the jump, but they knew damned well they wouldn't survive if they stayed put.

Kennedy recognized that many MEA members were skittish about becoming members of a union, but he also knew that the vast majority of local MEA members would have started boiling tar and collecting feathers if MEA were to turn its back on collective bargaining. For over 150 years, devotion to professionalism at all costs had not worked for teachers in any practical way, and cotton-candy professionalism (the kind being dispensed by NEA at the national level) was a confection that teachers could no longer afford. Even the most anti-union MEA members were fed up with the status quo. Kennedy also knew that Michigan teachers had a clear and present alternative to MEA, namely the American Federation of Teachers.

At that time, MEA had about seventy thousand members, and AFT about fifteen thousand. If MEA had snubbed the collective-bargaining statute, without question tens of thousands of MEA members would have gone over to AFT. The American Federation of Teachers was a viable teacher union in Michigan and was the majority organization in Detroit as well as several smaller suburban and rural school districts. In addition to owning bona fide bargaining credentials, AFT was not the least bit confused about its union heritage or ideology.

Significant defections in Michigan from MEA to AFT would have placed thousands of converted teachers squarely in the camp of organized labor, and might well have prompted mass defections from NEA to AFT all across the country. In states with collective-bargaining laws, AFT would certainly have organized teachers by claiming that NEA's Michigan affiliate had rejected collective bargaining. That organizing tactic would have worked, because everyone knew of NEA's hostility toward the unionization of teachers.

If NEA had lost most or all of its Michigan affiliate, it would have been standing on a hill of sand. AFT was already the majority organization in many large, urban school districts: New York City; Detroit;

Boston; Cleveland; Pittsburgh; Philadelphia; Chicago; Washington, D.C.; and Atlanta, to name a few. When NEA state affiliates in Michigan, Connecticut, New Jersey, New York, Minnesota, Ohio, Wisconsin, and Massachusetts decided to shed their professional pin stripes to don union suits, it was of monumental importance because they forced NEA to shop for a new wardrobe as well.

Because Michigan's elected leaders and staff gained tremendous early collective-bargaining experience, over the next dozen years NEA state affiliates hired no less than twenty-one former MEA staffers to be their executive directors. Altogether during that period, about forty Michigan staffers took significant management and organizing positions with NEA or its state affiliates. It's easy to see how the friendly (mostly) moniker "Michigan Mafia" came to be applied within NEA to its cadre of Michiganders.

At the national level, two former MEA presidents, John Ryor and Keith Geiger, were later elected presidents of NEA, and two former MEA staff members, Terry Herndon and I, later became NEA executive directors. To put an even finer point on it, on two separate occasions former Michiganders served as NEA president and executive director at the same time: John Ryor and Terry Herndon were NEA president and executive director, respectively, from 1975 to 1979, and Keith Geiger and I held these positions from 1989 to 1996.

Despite my chauvinism about Michigan, that state was by no means alone in providing impetus to the movement. State associations in several other states that had enacted similar legislation around the same time also embraced collective-bargaining statutes with gusto. Wisconsin had passed a collective-bargaining law as far back as 1959 but had not pursued it; Connecticut, Massachusetts, and Michigan followed in 1965; Rhode Island in 1966; New York in 1967; New Jersey in 1968; and a cavalcade in 1969: Delaware, Maine, Maryland, Nebraska, Nevada, North Dakota, South Dakota, and Vermont. By 1978, thirty-one states had collective-bargaining statutes. Some states, like Ohio and California, bargained in many of their local school districts even before their state laws were enacted.

Collective bargaining gave teachers and their organizations something they had never before possessed: a degree of power and a voice in determining the course of their professional lives. Collective-bargaining laws essentially placed public school employees on an equal footing with school boards in determining their hours, wages, and working conditions. The process of collective bargaining for teachers is fairly straightforward.

Once an official bargaining representative for teachers in a school district is legally determined, school boards are mandated to negotiate with the union bargaining representative. Boards must sit across the negotiating table and receive and consider proposals from employee organizations. They cannot, under the law, refuse to share information or make top-down, unilateral decisions.

In the 1960s, free at last, teachers were no longer mendicants begging for leftovers, and collective-bargaining laws became their modern day Magna Carta. The collective-bargaining process establishes parity between labor and management on negotiable issues (wages, hours, and working conditions), and creates a set of norms and conventions for reaching agreement. The primary object of collective bargaining is for the parties to reach agreement first on a series of specific issues, and then ultimately to compile those agreements into a master contract that both parties pledge to live by and enforce. Collective bargaining not only produces tangible benefits for employees, but enables management to gain employee stability during the term of the mutual contract. When a strike occurs, it heralds the *failure* of the bargaining process.

CHAPTER 11

Unionization In, Administrators Out

During the collective-bargaining reformation of the '60s, burgeoning numbers of NEA members around the country abandoned the organization's fantasies of professionalism at all costs in order to embrace unionism. NEA members, particularly local leaders, had increasingly realized that their professional associations had neither the will nor the weaponry to change their pay and employment status for the better.

The only forceful action traditionally employed by professional associations was "sanctions," an activity with the speed of a caterpillar and the impact of a peashooter. Rarely imposed, sanctions were designed to highlight school districts or education systems that provided a grievously substandard education for students. If utilized, NEA sent a "sanctions alert" to colleges and universities all over America informing prospective teachers and administrators that they should not apply for jobs in the sanctioned district. NEA also denied use of its own education placement services.

It took a long time for the sanctions process to unfurl because a pattern of abuse had to be documented after a thorough investigation by a team of educators. Sanctions were the educational equivalent of shunning, and school districts abhorred them even more than strikes because they were a national embarrassment, and they publicly sullied the district's reputation. From NEA's perspective, sanctions were preferred over strikes because they carried the aura of professionalism and altruism, not merely self-serving pecuniary interests. Consequently, sanctions allowed NEA to remain untainted by the grunge of unionism. The advent of collective bargaining rendered sanctions useless. The process was far too slow to serve any useful purpose in a collective-bargaining context, and the last thing school districts or local associations needed was to have the lengthy and often emotional specter of sanctions hanging over the bargaining process.

The first few years (1965–1970) of local bargaining in most school districts around the country were extremely successful. Thousands of contracts came to fruition without much trouble as negotiators kept things in perspective. Where there were strikes, they often bespoke long-simmering frustrations. A few local unions (not many) went over the line as they tried to sweep away decades of neglect and mistreatment overnight. They allowed themselves to be seduced by the inherently adversarial nature of collective bargaining and tried to use the process to *punish* school boards instead of seeking solutions to problems. To them, agreement on a contract almost became a secondary goal.

Sometimes, in those early days, local teacher negotiators personalized the process by singling out the superintendent or a member of the school board for public opprobrium. They would do such things as picket the homes of these individuals or take out newspaper ads identifying them as the blockers to a contract settlement. I've never subscribed to personalization (i.e., singling out individuals) as a bargaining tactic. It's usually unnecessary and unfair, and it hardens the opposition.

For their part, most school boards accepted the new collective-bargaining laws and engaged in good-faith efforts to make them work. A small minority had to be dragged, kicking and screaming, into their new reality, however. Some school boards dug in their heels and declared that—bargaining law or no bargaining law—they intended to hold the line against any appreciable salary increases for teachers.

A few school boards even tried to break the local association, an exercise that virtually never worked. Those boards convinced themselves that the union's demands derived solely from the anarchical minds of a few union rabble-rousers. They rationalized that the teachers were unaware of their own negotiators' demands, and that once they found out they would rise up in anger and throw their leaders overboard. Superintendents who peddled this fairy tale to their boards simply could not bring themselves to believe that *their* teachers would strike because they would *never* condone unionism and collective bargaining.

Once in a while, a school board would communicate directly with the teachers about the board's positions and rationale at the bargaining table (a clear violation of the bargaining statutes), circumventing the teachers' bargaining team in the process. Such attempts never worked and always infuriated the union membership. It took a few school boards and superintendents several years to accept the reality that education's feudal system had come to an end. At least in collective-bargaining states, the plantation mentality of school boards had gone to seed.

At the local level, a fissure between administrators, particularly superintendents, and teachers began to widen, and school principals were caught right in the middle. These local collective-bargaining relationships stood in stark contrast to the dominant role administrators occupied within NEA itself. It was inevitable that NEA's cozy relationship with school administrators would promote rumblings among the rank-and-file teacher membership, and it did.

School administrators had been part and parcel of NEA's power structure from the organization's beginning in 1857. Not only that, but administrator organizations held the status of autonomous departments within NEA, each with its own staff, budget, and governance structure. They included the following organizations: the American Association of School Administrators, the National Association of Elementary School Principals, the National Association of Secondary School Principals, and the National Schools Public Relations Association. The teacher members of NEA were also organized into their own department: the Department of Classroom Teachers.

This all-inclusive structure was NEA's affirmation of the "education family." NEA administrator departments utilized NEA research and other services and occupied office space in the NEA headquarters building in Washington, D.C. In return, NEA gained curricula and other educational expertise from the administrators and enjoyed the benefit of having building principals in local school districts serve as the primary recruiting arm for NEA membership. It was an arrangement that was advantageous for NEA in many ways, especially in building its reputation as the representative of all American educators.

For many decades, school administrators had occupied the top rungs of the NEA's organizational ladder. Unbelievably, while teachers comprised 90 percent of the membership, administrators had occupied over

90 percent of NEA's leadership, staff, and committee positions. That was a situation increasingly difficult to defend.

The reasons for the skewed percentages of representation between teachers and administrators within NEA were explainable, if not justifiable. School administrators were the experts in analyzing education curricula and policy. Teachers, on the other hand, had been systemically excluded from those functions in their school districts and were not considered experts. Also, school administrators had flexibility in their work schedules, which enabled them to attend statewide and national NEA meetings; teachers did not. Finally, school administrators, particularly superintendents, had the "juice" within NEA to get appointed or elected to the choice posts; teachers did not.

The problem of administrator domination in NEA wasn't confined to governance (elected) positions. From the executive secretary down through the professional ranks, the NEA staff was heavily skewed toward school administration. Most of the NEA's executive staff were former school superintendents or principals. For NEA teacher members, the staff situation was a double whammy because teachers had to contend with the domination of school administrators not only in their local districts, but also within their own professional organizations at the state and national levels.

For over half a century, the NEA executive secretary and staff had been the controlling force within the organization, not only running things on a day-to-day basis, but also strongly influencing policymaking. The executive secretary was also the prime public face of NEA to the media and public. Because of an institutionalized president-elect system, NEA presidents and other officers came and went on an annual basis, while executive secretaries stayed on and on, their longevity assuring them power. Executive secretaries were not elected; they worked under contract to the organization.

From 1898 until my retirement in 2001, a span of 103 years, there had been 82 different NEA presidents, but only eight NEA executive secretaries/directors (not counting a one-year interim appointment). After Con-Con (the 1971 constitutional convention), the roles of staff generally, and of the executive director specifically, were made much more accountable to the elected leaders. Also, the NEA president became the chief spokesperson and public face of NEA.

NEA had spent the first hundred years of its existence establishing credibility in order to accomplish its mission of improving education and polishing the image of the teaching profession. Having school superintendents and other administrators occupy power positions within the organization produced tremendous cachet with the educational and political establishment, all the way from Congress and the White House to local school boards. That acquired reputation, however meritorious and well intentioned, accomplished much for public education in America but did little to improve the real lives of the vast majority of its members: teacher practitioners.

Despite the loss of thousands of school administrators as a result of its expanding commitment to collective bargaining, NEA membership grew steadily during the 1960s and '70s. By 1972, NEA affiliates were bargaining for members in 3,891 school districts out of a total of 3,911 that engaged in collective bargaining. The organization's membership soared from approximately 850,000 in 1966 to 1.5 million in 1973. Thirty years later it topped 2.5 million.

CHAPTER 12

Black and White Together

As if all that was going on in NEA with the collective-bargaining rev-olution wasn't enough, in 1966 another extremely important episode took place: the merger of NEA's black and white state affiliates in the South. Again, at the instigation of the representative assembly and ur-ban activists, NEA stepped up to the challenge, and did so during a rap-idly changing and tumultuous environment for the organization.

The merger of NEA and the American Teachers Association (ATA) was long overdue, but still represented a real feather in the cap of both organizations. It was yet another milestone in the long history of NEA's advocacy for the rights of women and minorities. America's teachers work hard to prevent intolerance from infecting students in public school classrooms, and from NEA's inception in 1857 the organization has battled racial discrimination. NEA admitted minorities into the or-ganization from day one, and by 1866 had amended its constitution to admit women as members.

In 1869, Emily Rice became the first woman vice president of the as-sociation, and, at its 1906 convention in Boston, Ella Flagg Young was elected the first female NEA president. Young was nominated from the floor, defeating the nominating committee's candidate. She cam-paigned on the radical idea that *teachers should be involved in educa-tion decision making*. NEA's first African American president, Eliza-beth Duncan Koontz, was elected in 1968.

The merger of NEA and ATA was special. In the South, black teach-ers had been prohibited by law from joining white organizations, and in 1904 John Robert Edward Lee, dean of the Academic Department of

Tuskegee Institute, created the National Colored Teachers Association, which became the American Teachers Association in 1937. Each ATA state association had its own membership, staff, buildings, constitutions, and programs.

ATA leaders constituted some of the most significant southern black education leaders and politicians: Mary McLeod Bethune, the first woman president of ATA in 1924 and founder of Bethune-Cookman College in Florida; H. C. Trenholm, ATA president in 1932 and former president of Alabama State University; and William Nathaniel Ridley, ATA president in 1945 and the first African American to receive a doctorate degree from a white southern university, the University of Virginia.

In 1947, NEA affiliated the eight black state education associations in the southern states and the District of Columbia, but those affiliates remained segregated and separate from NEA's southern white affiliates. During the late 1950s and into the 1960s, there was significant agitation within the NEA Representative Assemblies not only to end segregation in the South, but also to merge the black and white teachers organizations.

While NEA and ATA had been working closely together and cooperating on a wide variety of issues since 1925, the merger of the two organizations didn't occur until 1966 at the NEA Representative Assembly in Miami, Florida. ATA president R. J. Martin, NEA president Richard Batchelder, and NEA executive secretary Dr. William Carr officially signed the merger documents. I was a teacher delegate from Birmingham at that 1966 convention, and twenty years later, as NEA executive director at the 1986 Representative Assembly, I was privileged to participate in a reenactment of that signing.

The logistical and personality problems that arose during the implementation of the state NEA-ATA mergers were sometimes prodigious. Issues of finances, staffing, headquarters buildings, and who went where in the political pecking order were prominent and occasionally exasperating. Understandably, most of the black associations didn't want to lose their identity, and neither did they want a focus on the rights of black teachers compromised. Some of the white associations, on the other hand, were reluctant to move over and make room, and one or two were gnashing their teeth over being forced by NEA to integrate in the first place.

In addition to financial, societal, and organizational issues, the state mergers were complicated by the presence of several colossal egos of both colors among the executive secretaries of the merging southern affiliates. On the other hand, as arduous as that period was, there were outstanding leaders from both associations who made it their finest hour, and they ultimately carried the day. John Williams, NEA's Southeast Regional Director at the time, was especially helpful and productive.

The merged associations are now doing quite well, and over the last forty or fifty years NEA has maintained a close eye on minority involvement at all levels within the governance and staff ranks. While quotas are banned under provisions of the Landrum-Griffin Law, NEA tries in a variety of ways to ensure that women, blacks, Latinos, Asians, and Native Americans have every opportunity to take part in the organization's activities and leadership positions.

The organization's commitment to minority involvement is real, and the existence of a variety of human- and civil-rights activities, committees, awards, training, and programs attest to that fact. NEA has been a leader in the fight for women's rights, including the Equal Rights Amendment (ERA), and has also fought for the rights of gays and lesbians. It has had an administrative Division of Human and Civil Rights for decades, and the hiring of women and minorities into staff vacancies is assiduously monitored and continually encouraged.

CHAPTER 13

The Revolution Engulfs NEA

In the 1960s and early '70s, NEA was painted into a more militant corner by the increasing number of local and state affiliates jumping onto the collective-bargaining bandwagon. NEA initially responded to the rank-and-file call for collective bargaining much like Jacob Marley's ghost dragging great chains and heavy boxes through the halls of NEA while emitting doleful groans. Yet, considering its history and structure, and considering the degree of change that had to occur, the speed with which NEA adapted to collective bargaining and unionization was pretty amazing.

The impetus for unionization and collective bargaining fomented in NEA's urban locals, which were growing in number and influence. They pressured NEA Executive Secretary Dr. William Carr and his staff to address urban issues because even into the 1960s NEA had virtually no programs or projects designed to assist its urban affiliates, and it had little to offer in the way of collective bargaining. Although NEA was vaguely aware of the unique problems of teachers in large urban centers, it essentially ignored them. In the largest cities, particularly those where NEA did not have a viable local association (which was many of them), NEA had focused on signing up random, individual members.

Most of those individual urban members—many of them school administrators—were interested in NEA publications, insurance, or travel programs—not in organizing. In 1960, NEA had about 750 organized members in New York City, out of a teaching staff of 45,000. Meanwhile, AFT was organizing teachers in New York and other large urban cities into affiliates for the purpose of securing collective-bargaining rights. Over Dr. Carr's strenuous objections, in 1968 the NEA board of directors finally established an office of urban affairs.

In November 1960, something had happened in New York City that was of extraordinary significance to the future of both NEA and AFT. A referendum was held in the city on whether or not teachers wanted collective bargaining. At that time there were well over seventy different teacher organizations in the city, none of which were affiliated with NEA. The United Federation of Teachers (UFT) formed in 1960 as the result of a merger between the New York Teachers Guild and the High School Teachers Association. With help from AFT and AFL-CIO, UFT expanded its base by merging more and more of the disparate New York City teacher organizations into UFT.

The vote in the referendum was 3 to 1 in favor of collective bargaining, an overwhelming mandate, and an election was called for the spring of 1961 to determine which organization would represent the teachers. The election rules allowed any organization to get on the ballot if it could get 10 percent of the teachers to sign a petition. UFT clearly had the upper hand, but NEA, even though it sent staff into the city very late in the game, managed to cobble together several of the small teacher organizations that were not part of UFT, and met the required 10 percent showing.

NEA called its group TBO, the Teachers Bargaining Organization. The election for a bargaining representative took place on December 15, 1961, and UFT crunched NEA by over a two-to-one margin. That election sent a clear message to NEA that it was in big trouble in the cities if collective-bargaining elections were going to be held. The reasons for NEA's problems were that the organization had no firm commitment to bargaining, minimal bargaining credentials, no experienced organizers, and no significant membership presence in most of America's urban cities.

About that time, it dawned on NEA's upper echelon that most teachers either wanted collective bargaining or soon would, and not just those in the big cities of the Industrial Belt. Most frightening of all to the NEA hierarchy was the revelation that the AFT and AFL-CIO were serious threats to NEA. The revelation was even more distressing because Walter Reuther, then president of the AFL-CIO's Industrial Union Department (IUD), was planning to organize teachers big time, and he had selected New York City as the first test of his vision.

UFT and AFT, of course, benefited greatly from IUD's financial and organizational help in the New York City election, and NEA was left to wonder what was coming next from IUD, AFT, and AFL-CIO. While no one knew exactly what to do, one thing was certain: NEA began to get the message about organizing, collective bargaining, and unionism.

Predictably, as collective bargaining and unionism gained momentum within the association during the 1960s, there was a concurrent push from NEA's urban locals to modernize NEA. It had become clear to local and state collective-bargaining advocates around the country that NEA was ill structured for the new era of teacher advocacy and collective bargaining. The impetus for a constitutional convention began to take hold, and an NEA constitutional convention was, in fact, a plank in the platform of a 1968 candidate for NEA president, Janet Dean, a teacher leader from Dade County, Florida. Although Dean lost her race to Helen Bain, a Tennessee teacher activist, the idea of Con-Con, as it came to be called, was born. After several years of bobbing and weaving by the old guard within NEA, in 1971 a constitutional convention was convened in Fort Collins, Colorado.

About a thousand special delegates from NEA affiliates all over the country attended Con-Con. Their numbers had been carefully distributed to represent all political, geographic, and philosophical interests within the association. Their recommendations were to be forwarded to subsequent NEA representative assemblies for action. Among other issues, Con-Con addressed the burgeoning political problem of overrepresentation by school administrators within NEA. In that regard, the recommendation that ultimately emerged, and was adopted by the representative assembly two years later, was that school administrators and classroom teachers were to be represented on governance bodies in direct proportion to their membership numbers. That recommendation alone upended 116 years of administrator domination of NEA.

Con-Con also elevated the roles of NEA's *elected* leaders within the organization. It was determined that the president of the association—not the staff executive director—would be the primary NEA spokesperson. The NEA president would serve a two-year term with the opportunity to be elected for a second two-year term. Until the representative assembly adopted that recommendation in 1973, NEA presidents had been confined to a single one-year term, an arrangement that institutionalized having them pushed through a revolving door. That arrangement, of course, concentrated a great deal of power in the hands of NEA's executive secretary, a nonelected employee.

Since the inception of the position in 1898, NEA executive secretaries had been unaffected by term limits and remained in their jobs until they retired, resigned, or ossified. Besides changing the job's title from executive secretary to executive director, Con-Con redefined the position to have responsibility for employing staff, administering the association's program and budget, and advising NEA governance. The days of the executive secretary being the highly visible spokesperson who pretty much ran NEA were over.

Another change springing from Con-Con was the determination to provide representation for minorities within NEA governance. The association, long a champion of minority and women's rights, and wanting to solidify the previous merger of the black and white associations in the South, institutionalized minority representation on most governing bodies. Mandates were later changed to goals as NEA came under laws governing labor unions, specifically the Landrum-Griffin Act, but its commitment to minority representation has never wavered.

Con-Con didn't stop there. It recommended that elections for NEA governance positions be conducted by secret ballot. In so doing, it not only reaffirmed NEA's democratic process, but it also protected teachers from intimidation by school administrators or other internal factions. Con-Con also recommended that local elections of delegates to the annual representative assembly, the highest policy-making body in the organization, be conducted on a one-member, one-vote basis. More than any other single action, this move democratized the organization from the bottom up. The net result of all this stood in stark contrast to the version of democracy practiced by NEA's rival organization, AFT, which held open elections for officers, allowed slating of candidates, had no minority guarantees, and so on.

Finally, of great significance, Con-Con recommended membership unification at the local, state, and national levels. This meant that as members joined at any level of the organization (local, state, or national) they were mandated to join all three levels. Teachers, of course, retained the choice of whether or not to join the organization, but once joining they could no longer pick and choose from a three-tiered association smorgasbord.

Unification bound more than 10,000 NEA local and 53 state affiliates (including overseas, Puerto Rico, and the District of Columbia) together. It unified programs and services within the three levels of the organization, especially regarding collective bargaining, and provided NEA with financial stability it had never before experienced. Unification tied the three levels of the organization together financially, programmatically, and philosophically.

After the representative assembly adopted Con-Con's recommendations, the organization truly emerged from its antediluvian period. The teacher members of NEA had decided to do something about their utter powerlessness and were willing to take on school boards, legislatures, school administrators, and even their own professional associations to get some equity. Enough, they said, was enough. During a single decade from 1965 to 1975, the blink of an eye by NEA standards, teacher members converted NEA from a tea-and-crumpets organization to one that endorsed collective bargaining and advanced unionism for its members.

In the aftermath of Con-Con, despite appeals from some quarters for administrators to stay in the organization, most of them, especially in the collective-bargaining states, dropped their individual association memberships. No one could blame them, having been excluded from the collective-bargaining process and demoted within the association to boot. It had become increasingly clear to one and all that NEA's focus in the future would be on teachers and other nonadministrative public school employees. Seeing the handwriting on the wall, the administrator organizations pulled out of NEA and became independent.

Action by Con-Con and the Representative Assembly probably saved NEA, because the organization had been staring disaster in the face. NEA lost a lot of ground during the 1960s when Dr. Carr and other key NEA leaders remained in denial, not of the threat posed by AFT and AFL-CIO, but of their own membership's burning desire for change. Dr. Carr held fast to the notion that if there *had* to be collective bargaining, then by God NEA would bargain for superintendents and other administrators as well as teachers. He consequently pushed hard for state laws to include school superintendents in local bargaining units. In his mind, Dr. Carr was protecting teacher professionalism and the integrity of the education family.

In almost everyone else's mind, such a scheme was a sign of organizational dementia. Dr. Carr eventually had to abandon his bizarre notion, not because *he* recognized the absurdity of it, but because local school boards did. They refused to allow their superintendents to be members of the very bargaining unit they were negotiating against, while at the same time serving as the boards' representatives. Of course the school boards were absolutely right.

State and local affiliates, however, didn't wait around for NEA to get its house in order. Virtually all of them underwent radical organizational surgery to take advantage of state collective-bargaining statutes. They had to, because unlike at the national level, there was no time for dawdling. When local bargaining-representation elections were ordered, there was no time for esoteric debate. The elections were going to be won or lost, and local associations did not intend to lose.

The locals demanded help from their state associations, which in turn demanded help from NEA. Because the local association members and leaders were in no mood to wait, it was impossible for conservative state-level executive directors to stall the implementation of collective bargaining. They were simply in too close proximity to local leaders and members to get away with it. Virtually every time a state-affiliate executive director rejected collective bargaining, the members unceremoniously showed them the door.

At the national level, despite Carr's apprehensions, the 1960s saw more NEA leaders willing to respond to the collective-bargaining advocates and lower the drawbridge for them. In the process, two successive NEA executive secretaries retired or resigned when they could not protect their version of professionalism—in other words, the status quo. Both Dr. Carr (1952–1967) and Sam Lambert (1967–1972) fought a losing battle to water down collective-bargaining statutes and keep administrators in the association. By the early 1970s, in local associations all over America, the waters of collective bargaining and unionism overflowed their banks and carried a new breed of elected leaders and staff into positions of power within NEA.

I'm always amused when anti-union activists charge that teachers have been forced against their will to join unions and are then held captive by sleazy union bosses. As Colonel Potter in TV's *M*A*S*H* series would say: "Horsepucky!" If ever there was an organization that underwent transformational change from the bottom up, it was NEA. It was, and is, NEA *members* who did a radical makeover of their professional associations.

The unvarnished truth is that in the 1960s and '70s, association members turned their own organizations upside down and inside out. They democratized the organizations and instituted an advocate-oriented agenda, changing NEA's reality from a tea-and-crumpets professional association to a strong professional union. Then, for good measure, they rid themselves of the heavy-handed dominance of school administrators and staff within the organization.

The single decade from about 1965 to 1975 could well be the most definitive, traumatic, and crucial period in NEA's history. The association's metamorphosis was tumultuous within the organization and controversial throughout education. This intense period brought profound change to NEA, including leaders who were not confused about what "professionalism at any price" had cost America's teachers. These new leaders were determined that school employees would never again be shoved into a corner and ignored.

In many ways, the leaders of the revolution in the '60s and '70s, up and down the line, were largely responsible for the power and influence that NEA later achieved in the '80s and '90s. One way or another, those leaders, far too numerous to list, contributed significantly to NEA's metamorphosis. However, I want to highlight several of them.

Dr. William Carr was not only a formidable presence during the transformation period, but also an interesting character. During his reign, Dr. Carr could have been the poster boy for association leaders who ran organizations like arrogant captains of industry or imperious school superintendents. It was increasingly clear to NEA members that the ideology espoused by leaders like Dr. Carr did practically nothing to improve their salaries and working conditions. They had had enough of NEA's "pie in the sky" approach to professionalism, and they demanded change in their professional lives even if it meant radically changing their own professional organizations.

To most educators and politicians, Dr. Carr *was* NEA. His attitude about professionalism was typified by the fact that he did not allow anyone to call him *Mr.*, or *William*, and most certainly never *Bill*. He was *Dr.* Carr.

He held court in an NEA headquarters building that even looked like a school, with long, dimly lit corridors, tiled on both sides, rising from floor to ceiling. If lockers had been hung along the walls, it would have passed for a typical post–World War II high school.

Old-timers on the NEA staff told me that in the 1950s a school bell used to ring to start work in the morning, again at the beginning and end of the lunch break, and finally at the end of the work day. Dr. Carr would stand in the lobby of the NEA building every morning to greet employees as they came to work, and he was there again to see them off at the end of the day. He routinely roamed the halls of the NEA building turning off lights that had been left on. He was scholarly, conservative, highly respected by the political and international community, and was possessed of a cerebral kind of wit that could be absolutely charming.

Running the organization in a quintessentially top-down management style, Carr sometimes asked for advice, but never shared decision making. He was a key player in government and educational circles, and had a hand in much of the development of modern education. Carr was also an inveterate internationalist who was very much involved with the creation of the education arm of the United Nations—the United Nations Education, Scientific, and Cultural Organization (UNESCO). He also was one of the creators of The World Confederation of the Teaching Professions (WCOTP), the international professional organization with which NEA was affiliated, and he served as its first executive secretary.

On my first day on the job as NEA executive director in 1983, Dr. Carr, who was then in his eighties, called to say he'd like to drop by to wish me well. My secretary, a dedicated and resourceful woman who had been around for many years, told me to make sure I called him *Dr.* Carr because he never called anyone by their first name and didn't want anyone using his. When he came into the office, I shook his hand and said, "Bill, I can't tell you how much I appreciate your dropping by. It's really good to see you."

He stared at me for what seemed like half an hour and finally said, "Well, Mr. Cameron, I don't know how long you'll last as executive secretary, but at least you've got nerve." Then, with a twinkle in his eye, he said, "You know, maybe it's time I should be called Bill; when I worked here, everyone thought I was an arrogant son of a bitch, but now that I'm eighty-two, they think I'm cute."

Dr. Carr and I became good friends in spite of the gargantuan chasm between our political, social, and association philosophies. We both loved history and the National Education Association, and those common denominators became the mortar of our friendship. He had just finished writing a book about Benjamin Franklin called *The Oldest Delegate*. The book was about Franklin's role as a delegate to the American Constitutional Convention of 1787 when he was eighty-one years old. Carr loved to talk about Franklin and could recite an entire speech, complete with histrionics, at the drop of a hat. I invited him to address the NEA management staff about his book, and he mesmerized the audience of 120 or so for over an hour. I thought he was actually going to morph into Ben Franklin right before our eyes.

Dr. Carr had been a member of the stuffy Cosmos Club in Washington, D.C., since 1946. He was proud of his membership, in spite of the fact that the club prohibited women from being members. The Cosmos Club and Carr constituted a perfect match: old, elegant, and intellectual. When he retired as executive secretary in 1967, he exited through the back door just as the NEA activists were knocking down the front door.

Carr's fears about creeping unionism within NEA were, from his point of view, legitimate. He and other NEA leaders had lived through the highly publicized 1957 McClellan Committee investigations into corruption within the Teamsters Union, and had been exposed to sensational charges of linkage between some segments of organized labor and the mafia on one hand, and communism on the other. To boot, AFL-CIO was threatening to help AFT organize teachers away from NEA. Carr and his confederates were determined to fend off the unionization of teachers, but the only alternative they offered NEA members was to continue chanting the same old professional incantations year after year while awaiting divine deliverance.

After Dr. Carr's retirement in 1967, NEA hired Dr. Sam Lambert as his successor, and Lambert immediately and unhappily became embroiled in NEA's transformational maelstrom. Uncomfortable in the job from beginning to end, Lambert lasted five short years as executive director, resigning in 1972. Chaos during a period of organizational self-renewal requires a leader who is clearheaded about the organization's new direction and committed to it. Sam Lambert was neither, being often indecisive and constantly worried. He was a nice guy—mild mannered, amiable, and intelligent—who had walked into a hornet's nest.

On a personal level, he was the opposite side of the moon from Dr. Carr. While Carr had been buttoned up and fussy, often dining at the Cosmos Club, Lambert was down-to-earth and informal, choosing his luncheon cuisine at a drugstore a couple of blocks from the NEA building. Lambert had previously been NEA's director of research, the same path to the top traveled by Dr. Carr. He was a worrier, and while he paid lip service to NEA's romance with collective bargaining and unionism (which got him the job), he was never comfortable with either one.

In his first address to the representative assembly in 1967, Lambert talked about NEA's commitment to collective bargaining, minority concerns, and urban locals; he also acknowledged the rising militancy of the membership. Lambert's words came from his head, but not his heart. The truth was that he disdained confrontation, was uneasy at best with teacher militancy, could not let go of the idea of professionalism above remuneration, and abhorred the idea of administrators leaving NEA.

Even so, much organizational retooling was accomplished during Lambert's time in office: collective bargaining became the primary focus for most state affiliates, NEA's urban locals emerged as a political force, Con-Con convened and made its recommendations, the Uniserv staffing program was launched, the statewide Florida strike took place, and NEA's New York state affiliate merged with AFT to become part of AFL-CIO. As impressive as that list of accomplishments during Lambert's short administration is, events seemed to occur during his tenure almost in spite of him.

At least partly because of Lambert's tenuous leadership, political power struggles within NEA became rampant. Strong personalities and ideas, from both the staff and elected leadership, vied for prominence, not always in a constructive fashion. At the 1967 NEA Representative Assembly, someone, in all likelihood a staff member, distributed an anonymous, crudely drafted handout complete with a schematic chart, contending that, "Representatives of the Mormon Church have very carefully and systematically infiltrated the National Education Association. Their purpose seems to be directed toward controlling the multi-million-dollar operation of the NEA."

This scurrilous, albeit ineffectual, handout was clandestinely slipped under the hotel room doors of convention delegates. It listed twenty-one NEA staff as being either "Mormons," or "Obligated to a Mormon," or "Directed by a Mormon," or "Independent." Its aim was apparently to cause dissension in the ranks and cast Lambert, who was not a Mormon, as a leader who was being duped by others.

The whole thing went absolutely nowhere, of course, but it did provide a little comic relief at the time. Speculation was that the handout's author(s) sought to embarrass Lambert and cause him trouble, perhaps launched by someone who coveted his job. Over the years, the incident became shrouded in mystery and was retold many times, like an urban legend.

Lambert stepped down as NEA executive secretary after five frustrating years. He went out in a blaze of glory with a fiery speech at the 1972 representative assembly that finally liberated his pent-up frustrations about what was going on within NEA. He began the speech by stating, "This may be the last report I'll ever make to an NEA Representative Assembly. After I say what I *must* say, I may be unemployed. But, come what may, the things I am going to say here today are going to be the real gut feelings of Sam Lambert, and I don't really care what the personal consequences are."

In the speech, he castigated NEA's New York state affiliate for merging with AFT; railed against the union model of leadership that would soon unfold in New York; and hurled invectives at AFL-CIO generally and its president, George Meany, in particular. Amazingly, after having praised the Florida Education Association (FEA) leaders and the statewide walkout in dozens of previous speeches, he bitterly criticized FEA and the strike.

Then, for good measure, Lambert blasted Con-Con's recommendation to enhance the role of the NEA president while reducing the executive director's. He said, "A very powerful president and an executive director, substantially reduced in status, prestige, and authority, will require the executive director to support the politicians or his tenure will be very short."

I think it's safe to say that Lambert was angry. He was unhappy about the direction in which NEA was headed, and he was frustrated with his inability to control events and, in some cases, his own staff. His speech proved that he was right about at least *one* thing: he was out of a job. Within a few weeks after the speech, the NEA executive committee, after a closed-door session, accepted his resignation. Without question, Sam Lambert had been a tremulous ship's captain during stormy organizational seas.

As if Lambert didn't have enough trouble during his five-year stint, in 1969 and 1970 he had to contend with NEA president George Fischer, a teacher from Des Moines, Iowa. Fischer actually served more than one year as president because before beginning his own term he completed the last six months of his predecessor's. In 1968, Libby Koontz, a special-education teacher from Salisbury, North Carolina, had been elected NEA's first black president, but she left the NEA presidency in January 1969 to accept a post in the Nixon administration as head of the Women's Bureau of the Department of Labor. When Koontz stepped down, Fischer was not hesitant to take over; he was locked, loaded, and ready to go.

If anyone at NEA boldly personified where NEA was headed, it was George Fischer. If anyone at that time represented the emerging unionist sentiment within NEA, it was Fischer. Supremely self-confident (many say arrogant), and decidedly opinionated (some say insufferable), Fischer was on the cutting edge of NEA's rebirth and reveled in it. He was demonstrably different from virtually all his predecessors, who had served their single-year terms in office by flying under the radar screen. Fischer flew high.

He became NEA president in the days before NEA presidents had any institutional power, but that didn't stop him. He butted heads with practically everyone, and held bold opinions—opinions he reveled in telling everyone. Although constricted somewhat by NEA's culture of staff and administrator domination, Fischer made his presence known. Just about the time he assumed office in 1969, he became the center of a roaring contretemps within NEA because of an interview he had given to a local newspaper in Des Moines, Iowa, the interview being picked up and reprinted in newspapers all over the country. Among other things in the article, Fischer said, "I don't give a damn about ad-

ministrators and superintendents. If they were really leaders in education, we wouldn't need the NEA. All I care about is teachers."

This incident came at a time when school administrators were still in
control of most of NEA's operations. When asked if he thought the public would support his views, Fischer said, "I don't care if they do or not.
The public doesn't always support the right things, you know." I read
Fischer's interview in the *Detroit Free Press* while I was still in Michigan and was stunned but elated. I knew one thing was for sure: the shit
was going to hit the fan at NEA, and it did. Fischer found himself in a
passel of trouble with school administrators and their sympathizers
within NEA; there was even talk of impeachment. However, he weath-
ered the storm and finished his term(s) in office without immolating
himself before he even got started.

I saw his hubris firsthand when, in 1969, the Michigan Education
Association assigned me to provide public-relations help to a couple of
thousand teachers on strike in Flint, Michigan. After much chest beating and thrashing around by both parties during the strike, the teachers
and board of education ended up in court. The judge decided to medi-
ate a settlement of the dispute and sequestered the negotiators for both
sides in his chambers. After two or three hours of deliberations in the
judge's chambers, Fischer showed up in Flint. Wishing to take advantage of having the NEA president in town to support the strike, a news
conference was arranged for him outside the courthouse.

With all the cameras rolling, Fischer, with characteristic flair, admonished the school board to reach a fair and equitable settlement with
the striking members of the Flint Education Association and said that
NEA was behind the striking teachers 100 percent. About thirty minutes or so after the news conference ended and the klieg lights went off,
the judge emerged from his chambers to announce that the two sides
had reached a settlement. Everyone was elated, and in the midst of the
jubilation Fischer leaned over to me and said, "My presence here settled this thing. You know, the power of the NEA president is awesome.
This happens to me all the time." I wanted to believe he was kidding,
but I knew he wasn't.

Being so clearly in a transitional phase, and having gone through tumultuous times, NEA wanted to take its time finding the right replace-
ment for Lambert. In 1972, the NEA executive committee hired Allan

West as NEA's acting executive director. Allan Morrell West had been Lambert's deputy and the man who, as much as anyone else, had been responsible for NEA's turn toward more assertive representation for teacher members. He was a strong advocate for the burgeoning ranks of the more militant urban leaders within the association and a strong supporter of collective bargaining.

It was with West's help that a political group within NEA called the National Council of Urban Education Associations (NCUEA) became influential. He even created a staff position within NEA titled Urban Associations Consultant to work with NCUEA specifically, and with urban associations generally. This radical idea had been pushed by the representative assembly and board of directors over the objections of Carr and Lambert.

West was honest, straightforward, highly respected, well liked, and nearing retirement, a perfect choice to hold everything together until a new executive director could be named. It was Allan West who secured Carr's permission in 1965 to hire the New York law firm of Kaye Scholer (the firm assigned to Michigan) to assist NEA with a series of thorny issues and problems surrounding teacher collective bargaining. Carr later came to regret the decision to hire Kaye Scholer because the lawyers from the firm came to have considerable influence with NEA's state affiliates regarding collective bargaining and related issues.

The firm's activities made Carr very nervous because the lawyers were assertively helping NEA's rush toward collective-bargaining prowess at a much faster clip than he preferred. The firm's lawyers were also very popular within the collective-bargaining states. Carr threatened to fire the firm and was planning to do so until Fred Hipp, the revered executive director of the New Jersey Education Association, threatened to pull New Jersey out of NEA if Carr went through with his threat. Carr backed off, but the incident demonstrated his antipathy toward the whole idea of urban organizing, unionization, and collective bargaining. It wasn't the first or last time that NEA's New Jersey state affiliate, perennially querulous but always competent, made its presence known.

West was not a militant firebrand, which makes it even more interesting that he played such a pivotal role in NEA's turn toward unionism— especially since he came from the state of Utah, which no one could characterize as a unionist training camp. He had been the executive secretary of the Utah Education Association for sixteen years before joining the NEA staff in 1961. While Allan West may have had a conservative Mormon background, he was a progressive lifesaver during a very difficult period for the National Education Association. After his retirement he wrote a book entitled *The National Education Association: The Power Base for Education.*

Another monumentally significant player in NEA's revolutionary drama was Bob Chanin, a brilliant labor attorney who has served as general counsel of the National Education Association since 1967. Especially during the Carr, Lambert, and West years, Chanin's value to NEA was incalculable. He is highly intelligent, conscientious, and does not suffer fools well. He can be prickly and occasionally rubs some people the wrong way, but he is universally respected within and outside the organization. Chanin is insightful and extremely helpful, particularly when the organization is faced with a difficult legal or procedural situation.

While Chanin and I generally agreed on things and had a great relationship, we didn't see eye to eye on every issue, particularly regarding some aspects of NEA's merger discussions with AFT. Nevertheless, he was an invaluable advisor to me and countless others, and I considered myself fortunate that he was there. Our paths first crossed back in 1965, when Chanin came to Michigan as part of a cadre of New York lawyers hired by MEA and NEA to assist selected Michigan locals that were bargaining their first contract. Our careers converged in a much more meaningful way when I became assistant executive director of NEA in 1979.

In addition to being NEA general counsel, Chanin is also a senior partner in the prestigious Washington, D.C., labor law firm of Bredhoff and Kaiser, and is highly regarded within the legal community, even by his adversaries. His 1974 book, coauthored with Donald Wollett, *Law and Practice of Teacher Negotiations*, served as a virtual manual for teacher negotiators around the country during the years of NEA's transition. It was, in fact, Chanin who largely crafted the legal and policy framework for NEA's participation in the collective-bargaining era. He argued four cases before the U.S. Supreme Court; wrote an *amicus* brief in the University of Michigan affirmative action case; negotiated contracts; and assisted local and state affiliates in legal issues ranging from censorship, to civil rights, to school vouchers.

During the 1960s and '70s, when NEA was struggling to overcome bargaining-representation challenges from AFT all across the country, one of NEA's most effective organizing weapons was a three-member organizing team dubbed the "Flying Squad," formed in 1968. Ken Melley, a former Connecticut teacher and staff member, headed the team, which included Chip Tassone, a former Michigan staffer, and Chuck Bolden, a former Iowa teacher.

The Flying Squad was housed in Des Plaines, Illinois, but traveled nationwide. Ken and his staff were good at their jobs and met AFT face to face in crucial local bargaining-representation elections from coast to coast. NEA's Flying Squad functioned, in effect, as NEA's special-ops unit, providing on-the-ground expertise needed to win many elections and stem the AFT surge.

The team's first real challenge was in Denver, Colorado, where the Flying Squad literally ran the election for the state and local affiliate, emerging victorious. They went from there to win other elections in Wilmington, Delaware; Portland, Oregon; Buffalo, New York; and Phoenix, Arizona. They also helped win a major, high-stakes NEA victory in Hawaii, which has a single statewide school system. The Hawaii election in particular was bitterly contested with AFT.

Melley was a natural organizer, having honed his organizing and negotiations skills on the Connecticut Education Association staff. He was tenacious, knowledgeable, personable, and possessed of a knack for analyzing the weaknesses of the opponents and exploiting them. In 1984, Ken became NEA's director of political action. Having always been a political enthusiast and activist, Ken surprised no one when he succeeded beyond all expectations. In fact, many politicians and their staffs in Washington considered him the best political director of any public-sector organization in the country. It was under Ken's leadership that NEA burst onto the scene as a real force in American politics.

Following Allan West's stint as acting executive secretary, in 1973 the NEA executive committee decided to abandon altogether its tradition of hiring conservative, administrator-oriented executive directors. In its quest, the executive committee became deadlocked between two candidates: Gary Watts, NEA's talented director of field services and a protégé of West's, and Bob Phelps, executive director of the Pennsylvania State Education Association (PSEA).

To break the deadlock, the executive committee turned to Michigan to recruit Terry Herndon, MEA's young, union-oriented executive director. At the time he was hired by NEA as its new executive director (the title having been changed from executive secretary as a result of Con-Con), Herndon was only thirty-four years old.

Herndon held the NEA top staff post for ten years until he surprised virtually everyone by resigning in 1983 to pursue other career opportunities. As NEA executive director, Herndon was something entirely new to NEA: a bold, experienced union organizer with an extensive collective-bargaining background. In addition, he was highly intelligent, knowledgeable about education and politics, articulate, creative, and visionary. Herndon arrived in his new job at NEA just in time to inherit the seismic financial impact of the organizations' having lost all of its state affiliates in New York, Florida, Missouri, and Mississippi, as well as the NEA administrator departments.

New York had disaffiliated from NEA after merging with AFT, in violation of NEA policies, and NEA preemptively disaffiliated Florida for the same reason. Missouri was kicked out of NEA for failing to adopt the new unified-dues structure, and Mississippi was disaffiliated because it failed to merge with the black teachers organization in the state. In dealing with these and a variety of other thorny issues, Herndon led effectively and commanded a great deal of respect.

Among his other accomplishments, Herndon helped create, along with Jerry Wurf, president of the American Federation of State, County, and Municipal Employees (AFSCME), a new coalition called the Coalition of American Public Employees (CAPE). The coalition, under the leadership of NEA's Ralph Flynn, pushed hard but unsuccessfully for a federal collective-bargaining statute that would cover all American public employees. He greatly expanded NEA's political action arm (NEA-PAC), and in 1976 helped NEA endorse and elect its first-ever U.S. presidential candidate, Jimmy Carter. He was an inveterate advocate for a variety of civil-rights and peace initiatives.

Herndon had quality assistance in moving the professional/union agenda forward during those years, and he needed every bit of it. His deputy for some of that period, and right hand man for all of it, was

Mike Dunn, who was also NEA's chief financial staff person. Dunn not only had an accountant background, but also was indisputably honest and politically savvy. He was a boon to Herndon, the staff, and the NEA elected leaders, and he enjoyed the confidence of everyone who worked with him.

Herndon was also fortunate to have the services of Irma Kramer, a superb executive-level associate, who worked on governance and policy issues and doubled as the repository for much of the organization's institutional memory. Kramer was highly respected by both NEA's elected and staff leaders and kept that bridge in excellent repair. Well beyond those attributes, however, her intelligence, curiosity, and analytical mind made her an advisor of inestimable value.

Sam Ethridge was another key player during NEA's transition period. He was a highly respected civil-rights activist who helped NEA embellish its human-relations agenda at a time when the civil-rights movement for teachers and other Americans was at its most critical stage. Ethridge helped recruit many NEA minority staff and governance leaders, and was a mentor and role model for scores of minority staff and governance members throughout the organization.

In addition to overseeing a rapidly changing staff, Herndon served with two union-oriented NEA presidents right off the bat: Helen Wise from Pennsylvania (1974), and Jim Harris from Iowa (1975). Harris was the last of the one-year, one-term presidents under the old NEA constitution. In 1975, he ran for the first two-year presidential term under the new constitution but was defeated by John Ryor, a former Michigan state president who assumed office in 1976.

Ryor was the first NEA president under the new constitution to serve for more than a single year; he served four years (two two-year terms). When he successfully ran for NEA president in Los Angeles, California in 1975, I was on the Michigan staff and co-chaired his campaign. Ryor is considered by most association leaders to have been one of the shining governance lights in modern NEA history. He was an unabashed collective-bargaining advocate, smart as a whip, well read, handsome, and a superb leader. He had a distinguished career as a teacher and negotiator in Battle Creek, Michigan; then successively as MEA president, NEA executive committee member, and NEA president; and later as state executive director in both Illinois and Florida.

Before retiring as Florida executive director in 2001, Ryor was instrumental in pulling together a successful merger of the two rival state organizations in Florida, FTP-NEA (NEA) and FEA United (AFT), to form the new Florida Education Association (FEA). After almost thirty years of division, rivalry, and animus, the two Florida organizations reunited and committed to stay united. Successful state mergers with AFT counterparts have been rare in NEA. Only in the late 1990s, as the result of national merger discussions between NEA and AFT, were state mergers approved by NEA in Minnesota, Montana, and Florida.

CHAPTER 14

Taking a Walk in Florida

Of all the confrontations between teachers and the power structure during the turbulent '60s, none was more dramatic than the 1968 statewide strike by the Florida Education Association (FEA). Because of low taxation rates and gross neglect by the Florida legislature for many years, Florida's public schools had been reduced to shambles—its curricula substandard, its infrastructure an abomination, and its treatment of teachers deplorable.

Florida's sorry state of education was made even worse in 1966 when the good citizens of the state elected as their governor a character named Claude R. Kirk Jr., the state's first Republican governor in ninety-four years. Kirk was almost immediately dubbed "Claudius Maximus" by the media and other politicians because of his unpredictable, flamboyant, dictatorial, and often embarrassing political and personal style. He got elected by promising voters that he would cut taxes, maintain services, and improve the state's education system.

Whenever politicians offer their constituents promises that are clearly contradictory and illogical—like cutting taxes, maintaining services, and improving education—they are being deceitful at best and harmful at worst. When such politicians are pressed to explain exactly how they intend to accomplish such a financial contortion, they dissemble and dodge. The truth is that politicians of this stripe have but one objective, and that objective is to get elected.

They are after votes, not Nobel prizes for integrity, and they count on voters' inattention, naiveté, or gullibility. Kirk was a beauty; on one hand he appealed to citizens who cared about the gloomy state of

Florida education, but on the other hand (or, more accurately, from the other side of his mouth) he clung to the politically safe, conservative, political mantra of lowering taxes.

Florida was one of the lowest-taxed states in the country. It has a constitutional prohibition against a state income tax and keeps property taxes low. Florida's main tax revenue stream has always been the sales tax, which is aimed primarily at profligate tourists. For years, educators in Florida had been complaining loudly about the state's sub-par educational conditions. School districts and the legislature, however, were unwilling to produce the revenue necessary to improve education and increase teacher's salaries. FEA, on behalf of the local education associations, pushed the state legislature and governor to do right by Florida's students and teachers.

In 1968, FEA's main bone of contention with the governor and legislature was not over teacher salaries and working conditions, but improvements in the school curriculum. First, the teachers wanted kindergarten programs instituted throughout the state (there was no mandatory kindergarten program), and, second, they wanted increased state funding for special education. Kids in industrial-arts classes, special education, and a host of other "special" categories were being dramatically shortchanged in their education, and the state's educators wanted to do something about it. Because of their abysmal pay and working conditions, teachers had also been lobbying for a state collective-bargaining statute for public employees.

It was the state of Florida's unwillingness to providing a better education system for kids that had the teachers particularly steamed. They were so steamed, in fact, that in 1967 FEA placed the state under sanctions, meaning that an advisory was sent to educators all over the country warning them not to come to Florida to teach. In response to mounting pressure, on January 29, 1968, Governor Kirk called a special ten-day session of the state legislature to deal with the issues raised by FEA. He made it clear, however, that he would not allow taxes to be raised in order to pay for any education improvements.

After three weeks of wrangling, during which the legislature unsuccessfully tried to find a package that would be acceptable to Kirk, the legislature passed a $350 million education package that increased taxes on the sales of beer, liquor, and cigarettes. Exhausted, and frustrated with the governor, the legislators adjourned. Kirk, in an orgy of hyperbole, publicly renewed his promise to veto the tax package because it did not contain a referendum (which would have taken him off his no-tax-increase pledge at a time he was preparing to run for reelection). The governor's political rhetoric was belligerent, unhelpful, and incendiary.

It was clear that above all else Kirk's main concern was to avoid being accused of raising taxes. His campaign pledge to improve public education while cutting taxes was exposed as the fraud it was. When forced to choose between raising taxes and improving education, Kirk dumped education over the side without hesitation. In order to deflect criticism, he blamed FEA for the crises, claiming that its real agenda was to get collective bargaining.

Before flying off on a political junket to California as the strike began, Kirk announced to the media that, "The real story is this cancer, the union, and its failure to teach children. They're not interested in teaching children, they're interested in having a union." He made this specious allegation, mind you, in spite of the fact that the union had no power, no authority, no rights, and no salary demands before the legislature. It was true that for obvious reasons the embers of collective bargaining were glowing in Florida, but Kirk's rants about the union being uninterested in teaching children was a smoke screen.

Kirk's performance during the walkout was appalling. He blustered, he taunted, he fought with his own cabinet, he threatened the legislature and anyone else who disagreed with him, and he left the state. A few years ago, the *Miami Herald* published a thirty-year retrospective article by Robert Sanchez about the 1968 statewide teacher strike. In discussing the governor's absence from the state at the time of the walkout, Sanchez wrote, "Finally, on Wednesday of the strike's first week, Governor Kirk flew back to Florida and on to Miami to confront the Dade Classroom Teachers Association (Dade CTA)."

"The CTA, led by Janet Dean and Pat Tornillo, was conducting nightly pep rallies at Miami's Marine Stadium. 'Claudius Maximus' arrived by helicopter at 8:23 P.M. As he moved toward the rostrum, he asked Perry [his education advisor], 'What's the longest Castro ever talked?' Perry said he didn't know. 'Find out,' Kirk bellowed. Perry asked Channel 4 newsman Manolo Reyes and was told that Castro's record for verbosity was 'something like two hours and 54 minutes.' Perry then informed Kirk. 'Set your watch!' the Governor bellowed, and began talking. And talking. Finally, at 11:22, Kirk eclipsed Castro's record, quit talking, turned to Perry, and announced: 'We beat that Commie S.O.B.'"

As a result of the legislature's modest tax package, which FEA considered inadequate, and Kirk's promised veto of even that compromise, the Florida Education Association called for a statewide walkout of educators to begin on February 19, 1968, if the governor refused to sign the legislation. Kirk refused, and on that day about thirty-five thousand Florida teachers left their classrooms, and over a million students were out of school. On the day the strike began, the media photographed "Claudius Maximus" at California's Disneyland shaking hands with Goofy.

However noble its intention, the Florida Education Association was in over its head. It was no more equipped to handle such an undertaking than a troop of boy scouts. NEA struggled mightily to provide assistance to FEA and its members, quickly determining to spend whatever it took to get the job done and worry about the tab later (over $2 million). FEA's saving grace, made possible by NEA, was access to a plethora of young, energetic, experienced negotiators and staff organizers from collective-bargaining states like Michigan, Connecticut, Wisconsin, New York, New Jersey, Pennsylvania, and others.

NEA sent out the call to state and local affiliates around the country asking for staff to be released so they could head to Florida. As executive director of the Birmingham Education Association, I was asked by NEA and MEA to go to Florida, and I did so after securing the enthusiastic approval of the Birmingham Education Association board of directors. They also approved BEA's president, John Dunlop, to join me.

So, off we flew to Florida, two wizened bargaining veterans of two years, ready and eager to help however we could. Along with a hundred or so other staffers from around the country who flew in at different times over the next two weeks, we took wing to Orlando, where FEA and NEA had established a briefing headquarters for incoming staff. After being apprised of the situation by FEA and NEA leaders, we were immediately dispatched to different parts of the state: Dunlop to Duval, and me to Orange and Brevard Counties.

During the three weeks of the walkout, the courage demonstrated by the striking educators made my heart go out to them, especially given the fearsome powers they faced. The striking teachers believed strongly in what they were doing, but many of them were scared silly, and their fears escalated as school boards and superintendents constantly threatened them with losing their jobs if they didn't return to work. The only viable protection the striking teachers had was to stick together like a herd of gazelles on the Serengeti Plain—a tenuous strategy, prone to having individual members picked off one at a time. Their adopted motto became, "No one goes back until everyone goes back," but that was easier said than done.

Every day, in every county, striking teachers would meet in general session to get briefed, but every day there were more and more empty seats in the audience. In an effort to shore up the erosion of striking members returning to school, leaders in many counties asked their constituents to sit in the same seats at every meeting and establish a bond with their neighbors on both sides.

In one county, the school board had obtained an injunction prohibiting their teachers from meeting collectively to discuss the strike. The injunction was intended to prevent the strikers from coordinating and planning their activities during the walkout, but it also deprived them of the security generated from being together. The day after the injunction was issued, the teachers gathered for their daily briefing while local police stood in the back of the room. Unsure of what was going to happen with the police presence, the association president began to speak to the thousands of teachers present about the walkout and was arrested.

Spontaneously, as the president was led away, the vice president went to the microphone to continue the briefing and was also led off by the police; then the secretary-treasurer followed suit with the same result; then came the members of the executive committee one at a time. As each leader was led away, the crowd stood and applauded. After eight or nine of these arrests, the police gave up and closed down the meeting.

At a county where I was assigned, just prior to one of the daily gatherings, two young married couples that I had met earlier in the week were talking in the corner of the auditorium. The women were crying. They told me that the previous day each of the two young men had received a call from the local draft board informing them that their draft status would be reclassified to 1-A if they were not in school the following day.

The walkout occurred during the height of the Vietnam War, and the two couples had been up most of the night talking about what they should do. They told me that both families had decided to remain on strike. Male teachers in other counties were also threatened with draft reclassifications. It was obvious that what motivated these teachers wasn't money or power. They really believed they could give Florida students a better education. Their strength and convictions amazed me then and amaze me now.

During the walkout, a local leader named Marge Head was president of the five-thousand-member Broward Classroom Teachers Association (Broward CTA). When the statewide strike began, Broward teachers faced a dilemma, because while they wanted to support their colleagues around the state, they had just been on strike a year earlier. The Broward CTA opted not to participate, but Marge and about five hundred of her colleagues decided to join the walkout anyway.

Broward County kept its schools open, and as the days passed most of those who struck returned to their classrooms; however, seventy-four of them remained away from their classrooms for the duration of the walkout. When the strike ended, the Broward School Board fired all seventy-four teachers. Marge left the state and went to Hattiesburg, Mississippi, to teach school.

In 1972, as a result of NEA lawsuits and several court appearances seeking reemployment of the Broward seventy-four, the Broward School Board agreed to reemploy all of the fired strikers if they reapplied for a position. The principal at Marge's old school offered her a job, and she agreed to return. In 1975, Marge was again elected president of the Broward CTA, and when negotiations with the school board over salary increases broke down, she led them out on strike again. She was, and is, a superb leader as well as a courageous and principled woman.

As the walkout wore on, FEA was unable to stop the slow but steady attrition of its membership force. Between returning strikers and "scabs" hired by school boards to teach classes, the position of FEA rapidly became untenable. After three weeks, the strike crumbled completely when the Dade County Classroom Teachers Association, led by its executive, Pat Tornillo, cut a deal with the Dade County School Board that guaranteed no firings. As a result, without consulting FEA or county leaders, Dade CTA unilaterally ended its walkout. Given this turn of events, other locals caved in one by one.

FEA, standing on a hill of sand and having been assured that Governor Kirk would allow the legislature's bills to become law without his signature, called off the statewide strike. Kirk agreed to let the legislature's tax package become law because he technically kept his pledge not to raise taxes; even better, he could blame the legislature and FEA. Each local association was left on its own to ensure the return of all its members to the classroom. Some school districts were magnanimous in taking the strikers, including some courageous principals, back into the fold. Other counties, like Pinellas and Broward, demanded a pound of flesh and fired strike leaders. Scores of Florida teachers lost their jobs, and teacher morale sunk to greater depths than ever.

By any traditional definition, the three-week statewide walkout was a failure for the FEA and the roughly thirty-five thousand members who participated in it, even though NEA and state affiliates had poured millions of dollars into the effort. In terms of tangible results, it produced virtually no immediate improvements in school curricula, working conditions, or teachers' salaries over what the state legislature had offered prior to the strike. Many teachers and administrators lost their jobs, and many never outlived the trauma of the whole experience.

Despite all that, the strike did accomplish several less tangible results. For one thing, it proved that teachers were willing to stand up for themselves and the children they taught—even in a nonbargaining state. Florida's teachers had defied a spineless legislature and a supercilious governor in order to expose the inadequacies of Florida's education system. The Florida walkout was the first sustained statewide teacher strike in history, and teachers around the country noticed. Most of all, it was another shot across the bow of America's education and political establishment and served notice that teachers were not only fed up, they were organizing—even in the South.

The firing of hundreds of association leaders and principals by some school boards resulted in lawsuits and recriminations, and the strike greatly increased the trepidations of school administrators about their future within NEA's education family. Because of the rising tide of collective bargaining in the states, and because of the increased militancy of teachers generally, school administrators became very concerned about their standing in the organization. They understandably felt caught in the middle and vulnerable within the very organization they had so long dominated.

FEA and NEA lost tens of thousands of members in the strike's fallout, including ten thousand in Dade County alone when Dade CTA jumped ship and went to the American Federation of Teachers. On the heels of the unsuccessful walkout, AFT had come into the state with a substantial organizing effort and gained a strong foothold in several counties, with Dade County as its flagship local. That circumstance set off rancorous competition between NEA and AFT, the two organizations that endured for the next thirty-three years. The organizational food fight was going strong when I went to Florida as executive director of FTP-NEA eight years later in 1976.

The Florida power structure did not escape the walkout unscathed. Claude Kirk exited as a one-term mortification for the state, and the legislature engaged in serious internal finger-pointing and blame fixing — all politically motivated, of course. The educational problems of the state of Florida were hung out for the entire nation to view, and, ironically, the strike led directly to the passage of a collective-bargaining statute for Florida's public employees by the state legislature in 1974 — the one thing the governor swore would never happen.

What made the entire affair so tragic was that none of it had to happen. If Kirk had kept his campaign promise to improve public education in Florida, the teachers would never have walked out. If the legislature had stood up to Kirk, the schools may never have closed. The indisputable fact is that, after all Kirk's huffing, puffing, and blowing, his clumsy impersonation of Huey Long brought embarrassment to hundreds of thousands of Floridians.

CHAPTER 15

NEA and AFT Clash

Throughout the '60s, '70s, and '80s, NEA and AFT locked horns in a life-and-death struggle for union membership. Usually, but not always, that competition took the form of hand-to-hand campaign combat in local bargaining-representation elections. Since only an authorized representative could negotiate for each category of employees (teachers or support personnel) in each local school district, the outcome of every representation election was critical. Both NEA and AFT had a lot at stake.

There were two ways to determine which organization would represent the employees in any bargaining unit. If only one organization existed in the district, *or* if a competing minority organization could not demonstrate that it enrolled at least 20 percent of the employees as members, the school board could simply stipulate the demonstrated majority organization as the bargaining representative. NEA had a big advantage in stipulations because in most suburban and rural districts it had existed without much, if any, AFT competition. The reverse was true in many large, urban cities.

If, on the other hand, each of the competing organizations enrolled a sufficient number of members to meet the 20 percent threshold, an election was conducted under the auspices of the state's public-employees-relation board. The winner of that election was then certified as the exclusive bargaining representative for the duration of the contract negotiated by that winner, usually one to three years. The losing organization was left to lick its wounds, criticize the winner, and enroll members during its period of banishment — a difficult task. NEA and AFT engaged in hand-to-hand combat in many large and small urban districts throughout the country.

The losing organization lost more than just the election, because it almost always lost a significant number of members as well. Those who belonged to the losing organization often felt an obligation to join and support the majority organization that was negotiating against the school board on their behalf. The minority organization held no power, and since teachers could hardly afford to pay dues to both competing unions, the group out of power generally atrophied and sometimes perished. Once a local affiliate of either NEA or AFT lost a local bargaining-representation election, it became exceedingly difficult to unseat the incumbent organization later on. Over the years, both sides tried mightily to do so, however.

For a twenty-year period, from the 1960s through the 1980s, competition between NEA and AFT took place from one coast to the other at a blistering pace. NEA and AFT pummeled each other with vitriolic campaign literature, and bargaining-representation elections were costly and exhausting. The two unions thundered toward each other like knights on horseback, each determined to crush the other. In those contests, especially when the election campaigns went on for months, the rhetoric became more heated, and interorganizational animosities deepened.

State collective-bargaining laws didn't just allow for the representation of teachers; they applied to other public school employees as well. It was inevitable, then, that both NEA and AFT would seek bargaining rights for nonteaching public school employees. Each group of employees had to have its own bargaining unit in order to ensure that the group's "community of interest" was protected. In other words, teachers could not be in the same bargaining unit as school support personnel like custodians, bus drivers, secretaries, and cafeteria workers.

NEA calls its nonteacher members *Education Support Personnel*, or ESPs. AFT calls theirs *Paraprofessional and School Related Personnel* or PSRPs. Over the last forty years, NEA has confined its organizing activities to employees who work *in* or *for* the public schools, colleges, and universities. AFT, on the other hand, organizes all public employees, including those who work outside the public schools, such as state government employees, state health workers, social workers, and the like.

After most of the organizing dust settled, NEA emerged as the larger of the two organizations by far. In 2004, NEA had about 2.7 million members, all of whom are employed in or by public schools, and AFT had about a million members, some of whom are not public school employees. NEA spent something like $25 million in cash, grants, and special projects fighting AFT in bargaining-representation elections over the previous twenty-five years, and that doesn't count what the state and local associations spent, which was considerably more.

Without question, the competition between the two unions drained a colossal amount of time, money, and energy away from each organization, and served as distractions in their efforts to improve the lot of their members. Like a fever that had run its course, the competition finally cooled in the 1990s during merger discussions between NEA and AFT at the national level. Those discussions produced many state and local "no-raid" agreements between the two unions, holding existing union representation temporarily in place.

Unfortunately, the national merger discussions came to an abrupt halt in 1998 when the NEA Representative Assembly turned down a proposed merger agreement (which the AFT convention went on to approve). Since the failure of the merger effort, NEA and AFT have tried hard to stop the wasteful competition and cooperate with each other, particularly in the area of education reform. As a result of the no-raid agreements and attempts at cooperation, bargaining-representation elections between NEA and AFT for teacher units are no longer as common.

In the earliest days of the high-stakes competition between NEA and AFT (the later '60s and throughout the '70s), most of NEA's state and local affiliates, except for places like Michigan, Connecticut, and New Jersey, were not prepared to fight these organizing battles. For one thing, most of the state affiliates were still under the domination of their executive directors, most of whom were conservative former school administrators. Another reason was that their dues and budgets were insufficient to hire staff and launch membership-training programs in organizing and collective bargaining. It would take more than a decade for NEA's state and local affiliates to become relatively self-sufficient in the collective-bargaining arena. The Uniserv program, which provided local staff assistance to affiliates, was a tremendous help in that arena.

The state affiliates had no choice, really, but to change from their noncollective bargaining existence: the members clearly and determinedly wanted collective bargaining, and they didn't want to be sitting ducks for AFT organizers. The last thing in the world state associations wanted was to have teachers in bargaining-representation elections face the choice of NEA and no collective bargaining, or AFT and bargaining. Providing that choice would have been an unmitigated disaster for NEA affiliates, because the members would have chosen collective bargaining virtually every time.

In the earliest days of the teacher revolution, NEA found itself in deep water and sinking fast. During the period from 1968 to 1971, NEA lost out to AFT in the urban locals of Hartford and New Haven, Connecticut; Newark, New Jersey; Philadelphia, Pennsylvania; Washington, D.C.; Detroit, Michigan; and Cleveland, Ohio, among others. Fortunately, NEA found a way to stop the bleeding.

One of the most significant things NEA did in the late '60s and early '70s (as it got its own house in order) was to push its reluctant state affiliates to get on board with collective bargaining. This strategy was necessary for two reasons: first, locals in foot-dragging state affiliates were bypassing the state affiliates and demanding direct assistance from NEA; and second, AFT was not waiting around for NEA affiliates to make up their organizational minds.

Another key NEA action was to hire a significant number of organizers, most of them in their late twenties or early thirties, who had gained organizing and bargaining experience in the early collective-bargaining states. Scores of those talented, early organizers are part of NEA lore: Ken Law, Ken Melley, John Dunlop, Ralph Flynn, Gary Watts, Larry Sorensen, Chip Tassone, Dale Robinson, Terry Herndon, Harvey Zorbaugh, Morris Andrews, Chuck Bolden, Jimmy Williams, Ray Edwards, Gene Preston, Larry Billups, and Arnold Erickson, to name just a few.

The American Federation of Teachers was a formidable adversary. AFT was born in 1916, fifty-nine years after NEA, when a handful of teachers came together in Winnetka, Illinois, to form a new national organization, one that would advocate for its members in strong local unions affiliated with the labor movement. AFT is very proud of its affiliation with, and active participation in, organized labor (i.e., AFL-

CIO). From its inception, AFT has viewed affiliation with organized labor as a vital element in providing school employees with the strength and clout they need to survive and thrive. Among other reasons, AFT was born because NEA was far too conservative and far too isolated from organized labor.

Over the years, AFT has had many fine presidents, but I had the privilege of working with (and against) both Al Shanker and Sandy Feldman. Shanker was a remarkable leader and intellectual who was held in the highest esteem by AFT leaders and members. Working with Feldman, I always admired her dedication to unionism and, even more so, her devotion to children, learning, and public education. During the years of merger discussions between NEA and AFT, Sandy and I became friends. The same is true of AFT's current president, Ed McElroy, who, in addition to his Irish wit and no-nonsense organizational skills, possesses the added quality of being a golfer.

Shanker began his career in New York and led the New York Teachers Union (UFT) through many difficult and dangerous times. When he later became president of AFT, he was thrust onto the national stage during the education-reform movement following the *Nation at Risk* report of 1983, and he made the most of it. Prior to his death in February 1997, Shanker became known as an outspoken leader, intellectual, visionary, and reformer, all fitting descriptions to one degree or another. He was the kind of leader who loved to engage people with the power of ideas instead of the power of office, and his contemporaries within AFT loved and revered him.

Shanker came from the old "It's easier to receive forgiveness than get permission" school of leadership. As AFT president, he often made controversial public pronouncements about teachers, teaching, public policy, and education reform, and on rare occasions would commit AFT to a course of action without having first consulted with his fellow leaders. Members of the AFT executive council would challenge him when that happened, but Al was usually able to convince them to come over to his position. If he couldn't, he would simply promise the executive council to be more inclusive before sounding off next time.

Reformers and school critics often lauded Shanker for his stances on education reform. He gained a reputation for being an educational statesman and, to an appreciable degree at least, was responsible for

AFT's escape from the "self-serving, union" label applied to NEA during the education-reform frenzy of the 1980s. During that decade, he enthusiastically endorsed the *Nation at Risk* report (NEA was neutral at best); called for higher standards for students (NEA did too, but opposed most standardized testing); endorsed a controversial plan to test all incoming teachers (NEA opposed); flirted with merit pay (NEA stridently opposed); advocated charter schools (NEA originally didn't); called for partnerships with the business community (NEA was ambivalent at best): and called for the establishment of a national teacher certification board (NEA reluctantly endorsed).

NEA leaders and members resented the amount of media coverage Shanker was getting in the '80s, but there was no getting around the fact that he adroitly positioned himself, and by extension AFT, as players in the education-reform movement. Not too long ago, I attended a panel discussion sponsored by the U.S. Department of Education on the topic, "Twenty Years After the *Nation at Risk* Report." Predictably, the conservatives on the panel claimed that there had been *no* progress in the intervening twenty years, and one of them, Checker Finn, a long-time critic of public education and teacher unions, placed the blame for the alleged lack of progress squarely on the shoulders of the teacher unions.

During the entire discussion, the only good word spoken from any of the panelists about teacher unions was a lonely comment offering that during the reform period Al Shanker had operated as a true statesman. Even that statement was quickly followed by the caveat that after Shanker's death AFT had fallen back into its old ways. While AFT and NEA had their differences about education reform in those days (they are much closer now), neither was responsible for blocking the recommendations of the *Nation at Risk* task force. NEA did, however, oppose some of President Reagan's policies regarding merit pay, abolition of the Department of Education, and school vouchers.

The *Nation at Risk* report of 1983 exacerbated the already existing animus between NEA and AFT rooted in bargaining-representation elections over the years. No small part of the increased hostility resulted directly from some of the public statements that Shanker made concerning education reform. NEA sometimes bristled at his statements, considering them to be inappropriate, untrue, or untimely. During those years, I gave many speeches castigating Shanker, but while disapproving of some of his rhetoric I totally agreed with his positive response to, and participation in, the national education-reform debate. I also thought his reaching out to the business and political communities was the right thing to do.

Shanker's public posture was exactly the kind of positive, high-visibility leadership that NEA should have provided but didn't. Mary Hatwood Futrell, NEA president at the time, was a superb speaker and charismatic representative of the organization, who had lots of good ideas, but her voice was woefully constrained by NEA policy and policy makers.

AFT consistently came across to the media and the public as innovative and flexible, while NEA was seen as defensive and predictable. Because NEA fought many high-profile battles to defeat school vouchers, beat back merit-pay initiatives, and safeguard teacher tenure, its education-reform positions were universally seen as defending the status quo, and its education-reform agenda was largely lost in the public din. While agreeing with NEA's formal policies, Futrell and I were both frustrated by NEA's unwillingness to experiment with change or try new strategies. Mary and her allies, including me, could not get NEA's internal political system to move very far.

I felt that NEA should have been more open-minded toward education-reform innovation. Because it wasn't, the organization lost a great chance to remold the traditional public-education culture. The time was ripe for NEA to connect with corporations, legislatures, entrepreneurs, coalitions, universities, and government agencies to challenge the systemic status quo. Initiatives were everywhere, the business community was engaged, and the system needed changing.

While neither Mary nor I agreed with every word of the *Nation at Risk* report in 1983, we did agree that most of the report presented an important challenge to America and its education system. We also agreed that the time was ripe for NEA to step out smartly with a positive response to the challenge, complete with NEA's suggestions and ideas for education reform in America. Unfortunately, we were both in for a rude awakening.

Staunch opposition to association initiatives came from a five-member majority of the nine-member NEA executive committee. They didn't believe that NEA should be leading, or even participating in, the surge for education reform. More specifically, they were adamantly opposed to NEA's participation in education-reform activities that did not comport entirely with existing organizational policies. During that period, Bob Chase, later to become NEA president, and John Wilson, NEA's current executive director, were leaders of that opposition bloc (both have subsequently had a change of heart in this regard, with Chase, during his tenure as president, boldly leading NEA deep into the education-reform movement).

The NEA executive committee is composed of the president, vice president, secretary-treasurer, and six members elected at large by the NEA annual representative assembly. In essence, the majority on the executive committee believed that most of the education-reform dialogue was empty rhetoric and a Trojan horse for merit pay. They saw merit pay and similar schemes as cutting away at the very foundation of salary equities that the association had worked so long and hard to acquire. They also viewed private- and religious-school vouchers as the unconstitutional death knell of public education in this country.

NEA was in a precarious public-relations position, because while the organization's prowess in contract negotiations, tenure, strikes, and political action was well established, its education agenda was not well known (contrast this to the first hundred years of NEA's existence, when it was an essential part of the education community). As its union-related activities increased, the organization focused less and less on the professional side of the education ledger—curriculum development, teacher training, testing, and the like. The perception that NEA was strictly a union that only cared about teacher pay and working conditions was exacerbated greatly after the release of the *Nation at Risk* report.

The NEA executive-committee majority demanded that NEA continue down the union agenda path. They wanted NEA to stand up to President Reagan's conservative education agenda of reduced education funding, elimination of the Department of Education, merit pay, and school vouchers, and they saw NEA involvement in education reform as a distraction from that focus. They were also concerned because many state governors, including Lamar Alexander in Tennessee, were agitating for merit pay in one form or another (Alexander called his version *career ladders*), and believed that if NEA showed any un-steadiness in opposing merit pay in all its forms, the organization would be seen as lending tacit support to it.

They also believed that the *Nation at Risk* report and its attendant publicity had no legs, and that this latest incarnation of education re-form was just another passing fad that would fade like a morning haze. They had every reason to believe that to be the case, because education-reform movements over the years had exhibited the same shelf life as hula hoops, pet rocks, and 3-D glasses. By 1985, we had all been "back to the basics" at least three or four times.

It's now quite clear that the executive-committee majority failed to grasp the significant staying power of this education-reform move-ment, which was powered by deep concerns in the business community about the globalization of the American economy and the dramatically increased skill levels needed by the American work force. Those con-cerns cast an enormous spotlight on the way American schools have traditionally operated, as well as on the quality of their education prod-uct. It didn't take long to discover that changes were necessary.

While Mary and I understood the feelings of the executive-committee majority, we didn't entirely agree with their analysis of the situation, and we didn't agree at all with their strategy of hunkering down. Our differ-ences of opinion with the executive committee led to some pretty heated debates, but we were rarely able to break through the stranglehold of those who were determined that NEA's best course of action was inaction.

Another problem NEA faced was that the staff was not sufficiently geared up to provide the kind of new and innovative programs required for full, positive participation in the reform debate. Again, this was largely due to the fact that since the mid-1960s, with the organization's emphasis on unionism and bargaining, an increasing proportion of NEA's program and budget had been devoted to economic and union issues. This problem didn't bother me, because I knew the staff could get up to speed very quickly once the policy issues were resolved (we were already gearing up behind the scenes).

For several years before *A Nation at Risk*, I had been advocating for NEA to bolster the professional side of its union programs and activi-ties. When making that pitch in two or three of NEA's larger and more militant collective-bargaining state affiliates, a few leaders accused me of turning my back on unionism, but those charges gained no traction because of my history with collective bargaining and union advocacy. In any event, immediately after *A Nation at Risk*, I scrambled to reorganize the staff and education programs to get them ready to go, which only added to the executive-committee majority's angst.

In order to understand how AFT's president could successfully tack his way through the howling winds of education reform while NEA's president could not, a word or two about the organizations' comparative structures and cultures is necessary. AFT's structure and culture essentially mirror those of traditional labor unions. Power rests largely with the union president, who is elected to office as part of a slate of candidates for top governance positions. When the union's slate of candidates is put together, everyone on that slate pledges allegiance to the presidential candidate; thus, once the slate is elected, those on the slate govern as a team.

Presidents within the AFT structure are elected for a two-year term; they can, however, run for reelection as many times as they please. When the election for AFT president is held at the AFT convention, delegates vote for a slate, not a series of independent candidates. Independent candidates can run, but their election is highly unlikely. AFT presidents know, therefore, that when they get elected they will be surrounded with political colleagues will be support their union philosophy.

Large local unions dominate AFT's structure as opposed to the dominance of state affiliates in NEA's. In AFT, state affiliates (if they exist at all) take a political backseat to large locals and the national organization. AFT local presidents and other officers are elected on slates in much the same manner as at the national level. Many of the presidents from large urban locals are elected to the AFT executive council *as part of the slate* headed by the AFT president, and, in that capacity, they also function as AFT vice presidents. The bottom line is that the president of AFT can reliably count on support from the executive council in good times and bad.

AFT local presidents are powerful, not only because they hold office for long periods of time, but also because they authoritatively represent substantial numbers of members in their locals. AFT places a high premium on strong individual leaders who are highly visible and outspoken, and tries to retain effective leaders for as long as they can. That means, of course, that some AFT leaders hold office for a long time. To cite one example, Pat Tornillo, executive vice president of the Dade County, Florida, AFT local, held office for thirty-five years until at age seventy-six he was caught with both hands in the union cookie jar up to his elbows. A hitch in the slammer finally got Tornillo out of office.

NEA, on the other hand, sees longevity in office as a negative, not a positive. The scandals involving long-term AFT local presidents in Washington, D.C., and Dade County, Florida, only serve to reinforce NEA's reservations about long-term presidents. That is the primary reason why the NEA constitution imposes term limits on NEA leaders and why the representative assembly continually reinforces that policy. The current term limit for NEA presidents, which is the most expansive ever adopted by the organization, is two three-year terms, a total of six years. NEA's cultural bias against individual power, as well as its insistence on term limits, has continued unabated regardless of the popularity or effectiveness of any particular NEA president.

To be sure, longevity in office doesn't necessarily breed corruption. Many excellent AFT local leaders have been in office for a long time and are scrupulously honest and still energetic. In practice, however, it takes death, a major scandal, stultifying incompetence, or public drooling to dislodge an incumbent AFT president at any level. Once in office, AFT presidents have a great deal of latitude to act within the general policies of the union. The AFT president is responsible for oversight of the union's governance, budget, staff, programs, and everything else. Unlike NEA, there is no executive-director position within AFT to manage staff and budget, although the AFT treasurer largely fills that roll on a day-to-day basis.

The National Education Association was created in 1857 by a small group of educators who gathered in Philadelphia, Pennsylvania, to form an independent, national organization that would "enhance education and advance the profession of teaching." It evolved over the next century or so into a strictly professional association that included school administrators in its ranks. Because it eschewed any relationship with unions or organized labor, it developed a structure and culture quite different from the union model.

NEA places a very high premium on its brand of internal democracy, and its structure is designed to keep decision making as close as possible to the membership. That's good for membership involvement, but the offset is that speed is hardly one of NEA's defining characteristics. With a bureaucratic structure rivaling the Chinese Army and the Catholic Church, its enormous size, its wide diversity of opinion, and its dependence on state affiliates to be the core of its operations, makes significant change agonizingly slow for NEA. Making significant change quickly is extremely difficult. Polar ice caps have melted with approximately the same speed it takes NEA to accomplish a major shift in policy.

NEA's decision-making speed is akin to an aircraft carrier in the middle of the ocean. It's big and powerful, but when a change of direction is required, it takes miles and miles of ocean to steer a new course. If, heaven forbid, NEA has to *reverse* direction, it requires more time than the life span of the crew. By comparison, AFT is not so encumbered. It's more like a PT boat, charging around the ocean with alacrity, changing direction quickly, able to reverse direction in less time than it took Al Shanker to give a speech.

For NEA, the tradeoff of democracy for speed is usually worth it. Democracy within NEA is truly remarkable, and the organization's structure provides maximum opportunity for membership involvement and input. The annual representative assembly, which is the backbone of NEA's body politic, is impressive by any standard. It has been operating as the highest governance body within NEA since 1920, and its control over the directions and policies of the organization is virtually absolute. Each year, more than ten thousand member delegates, elected by secret ballot on a one-person, one-vote basis from local and state associations, come together to set NEA policy and direction.

The representative assembly delegates take their responsibilities very seriously and spend countless hours studying and debating educational issues of the day. All delegates have the right and the opportunity to speak to any issue on the floor of the assembly, and during the course of the annual four-day meeting about two thousand of them do so. The NEA Representative Assembly has been the instigator and decider of every major issue NEA has ever undertaken: collective bargaining, Con-Con, minority rights within the organization, support for civil rights generally, the merger of NEA and ATA, support for women's rights and the ERA, initiatives to eradicate child abuse, presidential endorsements, and on and on. About one-third of the delegates turn over each year, leaving little chance for institutional stultification.

The NEA board of directors, the executive committee, the officers, and the staff cannot, and do not, operate outside representative assembly guidelines and mandates. NEA officers are elected at large, by secret ballot, by the representative assembly. Unlike other unions, term limits are imposed on NEA elected leaders, six years being the maximum any officer can serve in any one office. Also, the slating of candidates is not allowed. NEA is driven by policies that it believes come directly from the grass roots through the representative assembly.

Perhaps the most dramatic contrast between the governing philosophies of NEA and AFT is that NEA regards consolidating power in a single, high-profile leader with ambivalence at best and alarm at worst. It chooses instead to let the cumulative wisdom and strength of the organization, as expressed through its policies, represent NEA. It believes that no single leader should become the personification of the organization because it's not individual power that gets things done.

NEA expects its policies to be promulgated by its leaders on behalf of the organization. For an NEA president, or any other spokesperson, to draw too much attention to him- or herself at the expense of the organization, or to issue public statements that contradict organizational policy are real taboos. It's widely held within NEA that there is a plethora of good leaders who could be president, and any one of them could articulate the organization's policies very well. Another, infrequently discussed, reason for NEA's antipathy toward longevity in office is the fact that many leaders in the union's state and local affiliates aspire to top NEA leadership positions, and they have no intention of waiting a lifetime to satisfy their ambitions.

John Ryor (1975–1979) and Mary Futrell (1983–1987) were outstanding NEA presidents who were extremely popular. They were viewed by most of the leaders and members as extraordinary presidents. Yet, when Ryor tried to change the bylaws to allow him to run for a third term, the delegates to the NEA Representative Assembly turned him down. Mary Futrell didn't even try. Neither did Keith Geiger nor Bob Chase, also popular presidents.

My view is that term limits are a good thing, but the length of time a leader is in office must be sufficient to allow that leader to generate a national reputation and, more importantly, complete his or her agenda. At least eight years—possibly twelve—would be an ideal term limit. Perhaps that kind of extended term will evolve within NEA down the road. However, short of merger with AFT, which is unlikely in the near future, the chance of term limits being lengthened or removed altogether is extremely unlikely.

Because NEA officers, including the president, are not elected to office as part of a slate, there is little chance of a clique within NEA acquiring power. Quite the contrary, candidates for NEA president, vice president, and secretary-treasurer, as well as members of the executive committee and board of directors, run for office completely independently of each other, and don't necessarily share common education or union philosophies. Once elected, the officers and members of the executive committee may or may not form a close working team, and they may or may not have compatible political agendas.

In addition to other governance colleagues, the NEA president must work closely with an executive director. The NEA executive director is not elected, but is hired by the executive committee to work with the president and other governance leaders. The executive director is responsible to, and evaluated by, the NEA executive committee, not the president.

A differing governance culture is not the only characteristic separating NEA from other unions. On the staffing side, NEA's Uniserv (United Services) program is one of a kind and envied by most other public-sector unions. The Uniserv program began in 1970, during the halcyon days of the teacher revolution, and provides professional and support staff for every 1,200 NEA members right in their local school districts. These professional staffers are well trained in collective bargaining and contract implementation and also possess substantial organizing skills. They are distributed throughout the country in both bargaining and nonbargaining states. Financing for the Uniserv program is based on a formula shared by the local, state, and national associations.

Within five years of its inception, the Uniserv staff around the country numbered over one thousand strong. The Uniserv staffing program accomplishes several objectives: it gets immediate assistance to individual members who need help, it provides an ongoing cadre of organizing and bargaining experts to assist with membership recruitment and retention, and it serves to integrate the programs and services of all three levels of the association. Uniserv also provides jobs for talented association members who wish to become full-time union representatives, although having worked in a school district is not a requirement for being hired. Probably more than any other single program or initiative, the Uniserv program is responsible for NEA's sustained success with collective bargaining, political action, and member advocacy.

CHAPTER 16

The New York and Florida Tango

Of all the NEA and AFT confrontations that took place around the country over the thirty-year period from 1965 to 1995, none was more costly or organizationally significant than NEA's loss of its state affiliates in New York in 1972 and Florida in 1973. Both disaffiliations sprang from NEA state affiliates' unilaterally merging with AFT affiliates in premeditated defiance of NEA's constitution and bylaws. A three-decade ice age began as these state mergers generated tremendous acrimony between NEA and AFT.

In 1975 in the State of New York, one of the most traumatic and cataclysmic events of NEA's modern history took place. The telling of this tale requires a plethora of acronyms and initials, so let me help:

NEA *National Education Association* in Washington, D.C.

AFT *American Federation of Teachers* in Washington, D.C.

NYSTA *New York State Teachers Association*, NEA's state affiliate in New York prior to the state merger.

ESFT *Empire State Federation of Teachers*, AFT's state affiliate in New York prior to the state merger.

UFT *United Federation of Teachers*, AFT's local affiliate in the city of New York.

NYSUT *New York State United Teachers*, the name of the new, merged organization affiliated with AFT.

NYEA *New York Educators Association*, the name of the new state affiliate created by NEA after NYSUT disaffiliated from NEA (later renamed NEA/New York).

The story began in 1972 when NEA's state affiliate in New York, NYSTA, and AFT's New York state affiliate, ESFT—which included AFT's New York City local, UFT—merged. It was a merger that NEA didn't broker, endorse, or even participate in. The story ended with the entire merged state affiliate in New York pulling out of NEA altogether and becoming exclusively part of AFT and AFL-CIO. NEA lost well over one hundred thousand members in the state of New York virtually overnight when NYSUT left NEA, and NEA still holds Al Shanker, then UFT president, and Tom Hobart, then NYSTA president, responsible. In addition to NEA's losing its state affiliate and one hundred thousand members, the New York debacle poisoned the already brackish waters separating NEA and AFT.

NYSTA, NEA's state affiliate, had long been the dominant organization in New York, representing teachers in most local school districts throughout the state, except in New York City. Prior to the merger and subsequent disaffiliation, NYSTA was the bargaining representative for almost 750 of the 766 school districts in the state, while ESFT represented 10 (one of those ten, to be sure, was AFT's enormous New York City affiliate, UFT, which at that time had a membership somewhere around seventy-five thousand).

NYSTA's president, Tom Hobart, and Al Shanker, UFT's president, had agreed that the two competing organizations were dissipating their resources battling each other. They reasoned that together the two competing organizations would present a much more powerful and unified front to the New York legislature, local school boards, and the general public. The problems both organizations faced within the state of New York were serious, not the least of which was that the state was experiencing severe economic problems, and the potential for draconian cuts in education funding loomed large. Also of primary concern was the fear that the New York state legislature was about to come down hard on public-employee union strikes, and perhaps even curtail provisions of the state's recently adopted collective-bargaining statute.

The legislature was concerned about the power wielded by Shanker in New York City as the result of two teacher strikes there, the last of which, the Ocean Hill–Brownsville strike of 1968, transcended monetary issues and went right to the heart of who would run the New York City schools, the school board or community groups. The Ocean

Hill–Brownsville strike had strong racial overtones and ended with UFT's position essentially winning, but with Shanker going to jail— from which he emerged as the most powerful union leader in the city.

Both NEA and AFT affiliates in New York believed that their effectiveness in lobbying with the New York legislature was compromised because of their differing constituent bases. As in most states with a large and dominant urban center, politics within the New York state legislature revolved around satisfying the needs of political constituencies in the large cities, the suburbs, and rural areas. In the legislature, the fighting between urban and out-state interests often stymied the legislative efforts of both. Having two teacher unions pulling in opposite directions with approximately the same membership numbers, one representing a huge urban center and the other the rural and suburban districts, wasn't helping.

NYSTA and UFT leaders proceeded down the merger path even though serious, almost insurmountable, constitutional issues with NEA stood in the way, the most serious of which was affiliation with AFL-CIO. In spite of NEA's warnings to NYSTA that the merger being contemplated was prohibited by NEA's constitution and bylaws, NYSTA moved forward to consummate the creation of a new, merged state organization called the New York State United Teachers.

The merger called for NYSUT to affiliate with both NEA *and* AFL-CIO. AFL-CIO affiliation was in direct contravention of NEA's constitution and bylaws, but NYSUT technically met the requirements of NEA's bylaws because *all* NYSUT members were members of NEA and continued to pay full dues to NEA. All NYSUT members, then, were members of both NEA and AFT at the national level. However, no one really believed that this arrangement would last very long, because it wasn't realistic to ask New York members to pay double dues to two separate national organizations.

The merger dredged up other conflicts with NEA policy besides AFL-CIO affiliation: NEA required its affiliates to guarantee minority representation on all governance bodies, but NYSUT did not; NEA required secret-ballot election of officers, but NYSUT did not; NEA placed term limits on its officers, but NYSUT did not; and NEA had only public school members, but NYSUT did not. Predictably, each national organization defended its own culture and policies with almost pathological righteousness. Twenty years later, in 1998, those very same cultural and policy differences helped torpedo national merger discussions between NEA and AFT.

Those policy issues, while important in and of themselves, concealed an even larger problem, which was the severe political and personality clashes between NEA leaders on the one hand and NYSUT leaders on the other. Those issues had been festering beneath the surface since talk of a merger first began. Right from the beginning, NEA and NYSTA leaders simply did not trust each other. NEA believed that the leaders of its own state affiliate, NYSTA, planned to merge with AFT and then disaffiliate from NEA once the merger was in place. NYSTA, meanwhile, decided to merge whether NEA liked it or not, gambling that NEA would change its policies to accommodate the merger.

As a result of these positions, most of the dialogue that went back and forth between NEA and NYSTA about the merger became a charade. Both sides had predetermined where the other was headed, and developed organizational strategies accordingly — self-fulfilling prophecies. NEA and NYSTA's intractable positions spawned increasingly intemperate rhetoric.

Tom Hobart, NYSTA president and former guidance counselor from Buffalo, had decided that a merger in New York was in his own best interests as well as his organization's. Hobart had aspirations to become NEA president, and when that didn't work out, he saw an opportunity for expansion and extension of his New York presidency through merger.

Hobart also decided very early on that a merger in New York would have to include affiliation with AFL-CIO, a price he was more than willing to pay. His reasoning was influenced by the fact that AFL-CIO affiliation within the city of New York was then, and is now, critical if anything associated with labor was going to get done there. He also knew that a merger with UFT or AFT without AFL-CIO was impossible.

The New York merger was, by any rational standard, in the best interests of the members of the two organizations. If they had wanted to, the two national organizations could have figured out a way to make it work. They didn't want to. The animus between the two organizations was too toxic at the time, and the trust level among the leaders simply wasn't there. Consequently, New York members were forced to choose between

NEA and AFT. To this day, a significant number of NEA leaders at the local, state, and national levels believe that Hobart was more interested in
his own future than in keeping NYSTA's members under NEA's tent.
They believe that he deliberately handed NEA a "take it or leave it" ultimatum, believing he personally would win regardless of NEA's response.

Hobart had, indeed, made it clear to the NEA executive committee
and board of directors that if NEA would not, or could not, accommodate the New York merger, he would be forced to disaffiliate NYSUT
from NEA. NEA refused to be intimidated by NYSUT, UFT, or AFL-
CIO, and drew a line in the sand. Once committed to their respective
courses of action, the leaders of both organizations took the bits in their
teeth and thundered toward the finish line like wild-eyed racehorses.

NEA, on the other hand, believed that negotiations with Hobart were
destined to fail because he had already cut a deal with Shanker guaran-
teeing him a virtual lifetime position as president of NYSUT. NEA was
absolutely convinced that once the merger took place NYSUT would
disaffiliate from NEA and remain exclusively with AFT, thus avoiding
the double-dues problem and keeping Hobart in the presidency. Perhaps
NEA was paranoid, but NYSUT *did* disaffiliate from NEA, and Hobart
is still president of NYSUT thirty-five years later. A coincidence?

After the consummation of the New York merger, the stalemate between NYSUT and NEA went on for three years, during which time
tensions escalated. For example, NEA became alarmed that NYSUT
was promoting AFT in its publications while, at the same time, derid-
ing or ignoring NEA. NEA leaders didn't believe for one minute that
NYSUT intended to remain affiliated with NEA for very long, and they
assumed that NYSUT was negatively inoculating thousands of NEA
members in the state to alienate them from NEA prior to disaffiliation.

Seeing itself in an untenable position, NEA decided to go on the of-
fensive in New York. NEA president John Ryor and Executive Director Terry Herndon, in conjunction with the NEA executive committee
and without NYSUT's agreement, developed a media and service program for New York that was designed to promote NEA directly to the
New York membership, bypassing NYSUT. A series of NEA promo-
tional television ads were aired throughout the state. NEA, feeling it
had nothing to lose, aired the ads as a preemptive strike, hoping that at
least a percentage of New York members would choose to remain loyal

to NEA later on when NYSUT disaffiliated. NYSUT, of course, went postal.

The media campaign also paved the way for NEA to start a new state affiliate in New York once the NYSUT disaffiliation actually occurred. Matters were brought to a head in 1975 when NYSUT put before the delegates to its annual convention a motion to disaffiliate from NEA, and in March 1975, NYSUT delegates did, indeed, vote overwhelmingly to disaffiliate. As a member of the Michigan Education Association communications staff, MEA and NEA asked me to attend the NYSUT disaffiliation meeting as an observer and then help the nascent NEA state affiliate in New York with its start-up public relations.

The new New York state affiliate was called the New York Educators Association (NYEA), later changed to NEA–New York. NYEA's first president was Ed Robish, a teacher leader from Wappinger Falls, and its first executive director was Dan McKillip, a former NYSTA and NYSUT staff member who remained with NEA. The new organization pledged to organize fifty thousand members the first year, but despite NYEA and NEA's best efforts, and lots of money, NYEA membership hadn't reached fifty thousand almost thirty years later.

To a point, the merger problem in Florida followed a similar path. After the Florida Education Association's 1968 statewide strike collapsed in virtual ruins, the sixty-seven NEA local county affiliates began to split off in several directions: some defected to AFT, others remained loyal to NEA, and a few decided to be independent. In the fallout from the statewide strike, FEA stumbled along in a chaotic state for several years, trying desperately to put the pieces back together. The organization fired its executive director, Phil Constans; reorganized programs; and tried to rev up its organizing engine, but the slide continued.

Among other problems faced by FEA was that in the aftermath of the strike AFT came into the state and was organizing quite successfully. In fact, many locals left NEA and went over to AFT. Dade, the state's most populous county (and FEA's largest local affiliate) led the defection to AFT.

In 1973, spurred on by what was happening in New York, and for largely the same reasons, the NEA and AFT state affiliates in Florida decided to merge. The executive director of FEA at that time was

Richard Batchelder, who had been NEA president in 1966. "Batch," as he is known, was a charismatic and articulate leader who had gained the Florida job largely because of his reputation within NEA. The AFT power brokers in Florida were none other than Pat Tornillo, executive vice president of the AFT's Dade County affiliate, and Al Shanker, AFT president.

To fashion the merger, FEA and AFT cloned the New York model. That was no surprise to NEA because one of its issues with NYSUT was that while it was still affiliated with NEA, NYSUT had been sending organizers into other states, especially Florida, to organize for AFT—and using NEA dues money to do it. The merged organization in Florida was called Florida Education Association United (FEA/U), and NEA was once again faced with a "take it or leave it" ultimatum. Coming off the New York experience, and having the very same constitutional issues at play, NEA had forbidden the Florida merger unless there was total compliance with NEA's constitution and bylaws. Despite repeated warnings from NEA, the FEA and AFT leaders consummated the merger.

Florida merger proponents assumed, as in New York, that once they put the state merger in place, NEA had no choice but to figure out a way to accommodate it. To their amazement, however, having learned its lesson in New York, NEA didn't wait for FEA and AFT to get the strategic upper hand. NEA cut its losses by summarily disaffiliating the entire FEA/U state organization. Once again, NEA lost a bundle of members, about seventy-five thousand, virtually overnight; only this time, NEA was ahead of the organizing curve. Immediately after disaffiliating the merged state association, NEA organized a new state affiliate in Florida before FEA/U could lock up local affiliates.

NEA's new affiliate was originally named the Florida United Services Association (FUSA), later the Florida Teaching Profession (FTP), and still later FTP-NEA. The new state affiliate's engine sputtered for several months before getting started, but eventually kicked in. Over the next twenty years, FTP-NEA membership numbers became even larger than FEA/U's. Ironically, the wheel spun full circle as FTP-NEA and FEA/U successfully merged in 2000.

The New York and Florida experiences were not only traumatic and bitter, but a colossal waste of time, energy, and money. To be sure, both

NEA and AFT proved their points. In New York, NYSTA and UFT merged to become NYSUT, and that organization continues to this day, thirty-four years later, to function effectively. On the other hand, NEA achieved its goal of remaining independent from AFL-CIO.

Similarly, in Florida the state merger took place, and FEA/U, the merged affiliate, continued to function for twenty-seven years until it remerged in 2000 with FTP-NEA. NEA's new state association (FTP-NEA) had also blossomed and prospered until the 2000 merger. For almost thirty years, however, the two rivals in Florida pummeled each other unmercifully. The best that can be said about that confrontational period is that both organizations emerged bloody but unbowed.

Except for the true believers, almost everyone today would agree that the organizational trauma that the New York and Florida mergers engendered could have, and should have, been avoided. In the early 1970s, NEA could have found a way to accommodate the New York and Florida mergers if it had placed any value at all on the idea of affiliation with AFL-CIO—which it didn't. AFT could have operated in a less ham-handed fashion than it did in both New York and Florida by unilaterally handing NEA a fait accompli. In the 1990s, after all, NEA and AFT did figure out a way to make state mergers work in Minnesota, Florida, and Montana. It wasn't easy, and there was much weeping and gnashing of teeth before they became a reality, but it got done.

It got done because NEA and AFT leaders wanted it to get done. It got done because the two national organizations listened to their state affiliates and cooperated with them in finding solutions to merger issues *before* positions hardened and personalities took over. The issue of AFL-CIO affiliation is still the largest stumbling block to a merger, because to AFT the idea of existing outside AFL-CIO is unconscionable; AFT's very soul is rooted in organized labor. On the other hand, NEA's independence from organized labor is a long and fiercely held tradition based largely on three factors: professional independence; distaste for historical trade union corruption; and an unwillingness to turn power over to a single leader, especially for a prolonged period of time.

I've never been bothered by AFL-CIO affiliation and always believed that NEA and AFT could reach a creative accommodation on this issue. The existence of several merged state affiliates within NEA today proves the point, and, although not an ideal situation, it works for the states, while both NEA and AFT can live with it. In all three newly merged state affiliates, the state leaders were unflappable and courageous in dealing with each other and their national affiliates. They had to be because they lead the way, particularly Minnesota Education Association president Judy Schaubach and executive director Larry Wicks, Montana president Eric Feaver and executive director David Smith, and Florida president Maureen Dinnen and executive director John Ryor. As frontrunners, they took a lot of flack from the antimerger factions within NEA.

It is patently obvious that what it took to get from the *impossible* in New York and Florida over thirty years ago to the *possible* in Florida, Minnesota, and Montana in late '90s was trust and good faith between the leaders of both organizations at the national level. They were involved every step of the way. Specifically, NEA presidents Keith Geiger, Bob Chase, and I; AFT president Sandra Feldman; and AFT treasurer Ed McElroy worked tirelessly to make the merger a reality. Evelyn Temple, NEA's director of affiliate services, and Phil Kugler, her counterpart at AFT, were also an integral part of the effort, as was the NEA executive committee and the AFT executive council. The NEA and AFT leaders came to appreciate each other as people and were able to stop the interorganizational demagoguery that had reigned supreme for so many years.

CHAPTER 17

Off to Tallahassee

I went to Florida to become Florida Teaching Profession's (FTP) executive director in August 1976, just a year after having been promoted to the position of director of communications for the Michigan Education Association. When Terry Herndon left MEA to become the executive director of the National Education Association in 1973, his successor at MEA was Herman Coleman, MEA's first African American executive director and a terrific guy who had appointed me director of communications.

I had nicely settled into the new job when I received a call from Jimmy Williams, NEA's southeast regional director, asking me to go to Florida as the state's executive director. He said that the NEA state affiliate, FTP, which had only been in existence for a few years following the FEA–AFT Florida merger debacle, was in serious trouble. The FTP executive director, George Auzenne, had resigned suddenly amidst much turmoil, and the organization was floundering. It had only a few staff, approximately twenty thousand members and virtually no stability, and was $2.5 million in debt to NEA.

Florida's troubles were quite well known within NEA circles, and I wasn't eager to jump into the middle of them. Besides that, I had no desire to be a state executive director because it meant working directly for governance (executive committee, board of directors, officers—that sort of thing). As a result, I turned the offer down. A few days later Gary Watts, NEA's director of affiliate services, called and asked me to reconsider. He said that NEA had cut a deal with the FTP board of directors that allowed NEA to appoint, with their approval, a new executive director, a new assistant executive director for finance, and a new communications director.

Watts said that the NEA folks had talked it over and wanted someone who was good with people, had organizing and bargaining experience, and knew communications. I was flattered, but again turned the job down. Several days later, NEA executive director Terry Herndon, my old colleague and friend, called to add to the full-court press. He said he needed me to take the FTP job because NEA could very well lose the entire state to AFT if something wasn't done and done quickly. He also said that the NEA people involved were adamant that I was the person for the job.

After some soul-searching and discussions with Ida, we agreed to go to Florida. So in August of 1976, I headed to Tallahassee. The Florida Teaching Profession was only about three years old when I reported for work in August 1976. As I said earlier, NEA loyalists in Florida had created the new organization out of whole cloth after NEA disaffiliated the Florida Education Association for violating NEA merger policies. Four of NEA's largest local county affiliates in Florida led the way in creating the new NEA state affiliate: Broward (Ft. Lauderdale), Escambia (Pensacola), Pinellas (St. Petersburg), and Orange (Orlando). When the new organization was born, it had no governance, no staff, no structure, and no program.

The brand new organization was originally called the Florida United Services Association (FUSA). After a year or so, saner heads prevailed and the name was changed to the Florida Teaching Profession (FTP), which was only marginally better. Absolutely no one besides the organization's leaders had the foggiest notion of what the hell FUSA was, and only a few people could tell you what FTP stood for.

Even worse, when NEA disaffiliated its Florida affiliate, the AFT group kept the name Florida Education Association, calling itself Florida Education Association United. Almost everyone in the state knew the name Florida Education Association because of its hundred-year history and the statewide strike of 1968, but practically no one had heard of the Florida Teaching Profession. As the new NEA state affiliate was being formed, organizing battles between NEA and AFT for local-representation rights took place all over the state, and confusion reigned supreme because of all the different organizational names.

Some AFT locals still carried their old FEA names, and teachers in those AFT locals often thought they were NEA members.

Countless times we would go into AFT locals and ask teachers to sign up with NEA, only to have them look at us as if we were demented. With great certitude, the teachers would explain that they were already proud members of NEA and had been for years. When told that they were not NEA members but in fact belonged to AFT, they were incredulous. Given the rapid pace of organizational events, such confusion was understandable. Most often the teachers' loyalty was to their local leaders and local organization first and foremost.

By the time I got to Florida, the state association was a mess. There were a lot of really good, solid members and leaders, but they were crashing into each other like crazed slam dancers. Florida's large county-school districts meant large local associations, some of them with five thousand to fourteen thousand members. The executive directors and elected presidents who headed those large locals were very powerful people, each one carrying more clout individually than the leaders of the fledgling FTP state association. Turf wars erupted frequently, and debates about dues and programs (or lack of programs) were heated. It didn't help that relationships between FTP and some of its own local affiliates were not healthy.

The only common ground shared by virtually everyone was a visceral detestation of AFT generally and of Pat Tornillo, head of the Dade County (Miami) local, in particular. FTP leaders remembered how Tornillo had deserted the rest of Florida's teachers during the 1968 statewide strike and then had shamelessly defected to AFT when everything came tumbling down for FEA. He was viewed by NEA people back then as a publicity hound, arrogant, unsavory, and untrustworthy—mostly untrustworthy. They were right.

FTP had a skeletal state organization and staff in place and was headquartered in rented office space at the far north end of Tallahassee, several miles from the state capital. FEA/United occupied the former FEA headquarters building located just two short blocks from the capital. FTP was in debt to NEA for well over $2.5 million and had other debts as well. FTP's dues were way too low to get itself out of debt, hire staff, or get quality programs and services going.

As a result, FTP had to rely on NEA for virtually everything, a fact that presented a classic catch-22 situation for many FTP leaders. On the one hand, they didn't want to be totally dependent on NEA, but on the other hand they didn't want to raise their dues. The year before I got there, there had been a huge political fight at the FTP Representative Assembly over a proposed four-dollar dues increase (which would have accomplished virtually nothing). In the end, a two-dollar dues increase passed, which barely kept pace with the cost of maintaining *existing* services. That meant that NEA was forced to contribute even more money to provide for organizing, staff hires, and other necessities.

It was at that point that NEA intervened to create the financial package referred to earlier that brought a finance director, a communications director, and me to FTP. Only two or three professional staff members were actually employed by the state organization: a lobbyist, a research staffer, and a manager for field services. All the rest were on the NEA payroll, including six very young professional organizers. The biggest problem the organization faced, however, was its anonymity with the media, the government, and the public at large.

The organization had almost no political program. The FTP lobbyist was Tay Green, who had remained with NEA after the disaffiliation and was by far the best thing the organization had going for it. He had formerly been the top staff guy for the senate education committee in the state legislature, and a school administrator in Pensacola before that. My first day on the job, I asked Tay how much money FTP had in its political action (PAC) account. He replied, "Not much, I'm afraid; only about eleven." I said, "Well, at least we can do *something* with eleven thousand dollars." He said, "Not eleven thousand." I said, "You mean we only have eleven hundred dollars?" He said, "Don, we have eleven dollars."

In spite of all the organizational mayhem that had transpired in Florida over the previous eight years, including the statewide walkout, I was amazed that FTP had still managed to enroll about twenty-two thousand members. FEA/United had signed up about the same number, although they publicly claimed more than thirty thousand — which made the FTP people apoplectic. To me, the fact that fifty thousand teachers still belonged to *any* organization in Florida was a minor miracle.

In any event, FTP was saddled with the reality that FEA/U was getting almost all the media attention, as well as most of the consideration of state legislators when it came to education and legislation. FTP was struggling to be noticed, and the lack of name recognition pushed its leaders' heart rate into the red zone.

We tackled all these issues one at a time. I convened a meeting of the local executive directors to seek solidarity regarding the state association's legislative and political agenda. As a result of that meeting, and a lot of one-on-one schmoozing, we were able to bring the state and local affiliates together and, eventually, form a solid bond. Next, I convinced the members of the FTP budget and executive committees to recommend a twenty-six-dollar dues increase to the representative assembly the following spring.

They told me there was no way on earth a twenty-six-dollar dues increase would pass the board of directors, let alone the representative assembly. In order to gain leadership support, I had to promise to drown myself in a vat of boiled peanuts if they got into political trouble for supporting such a large dues increase. One elderly female teacher told me, "I'm sorry, young man, but that dues increase just isn't going to happen . . . bless your heart." I found out that when southerners say "bless your heart" like that, it often means that they consider you a piteous, childlike innocent beyond rescue (if they like you), or an insignificant, simple-minded microbe (if they don't). Assuming she liked me, I told her and the others that if we stood shoulder to shoulder and explained over and over exactly why the money was needed, and exactly how it would be spent, it would pass; the delegates would do the right thing.

I told them that our main selling point was the creation of a viable state organization that would effectively represent teachers, stand financially independent of NEA, and take on the battle with FEA/U and AFT. A whole bunch of courageous local and state leaders, including FTP president Carl Harner, climbed aboard, stayed together, and worked hard. The dues increase passed the executive committee, the board of directors, and then the representative assembly in the spring of 1977. FTP was off and running, and I didn't have to drown in a vat of boiled peanuts.

The dues increase allowed the organization to pay off the NEA debt three years earlier than scheduled, and enabled me to employ staff and build up the organization's services and programs. As far as FTP name recognition was concerned, we did several things. First, we added NEA to the organization's name so that it became FTP-NEA. Then I told the staff, "From this day forward, FTP-NEA is to declare over and over in press releases, speeches, public announcements, or whatever that FTP-NEA will be called 'Florida's Largest Teachers' Organization.'" And that's just what we did over the next few months.

It wasn't very long before the media began each mention of FTP-NEA with the tag "Florida's Largest Teachers' Organization." Just for fun, we tweaked FEA/U about our new motto whenever possible. For example, we rented prime billboard space at the Tallahassee airport with the new FTP-NEA slogan emblazoned across the whole thing so that anyone who came to Tallahassee to take a seat in the legislature, to lobby, or just to visit couldn't miss the sign. I also assigned six staff people, including myself, to lobby in the legislature during the sixty-day legislative session, and each one of us wore a large, gold, metal name tag that said in large letters: "FTP-NEA, Florida's Largest Teachers' Organization." They were attractive, but they were very large, about the size of a computer diskette. Pretty soon, people in general, and certainly legislators, recognized FTP-NEA as it grew into a viable state association.

Pushing my luck, I tried to get the FTP-NEA Representative Assembly to approve another name change for the organization: Florida NEA. The delegates turned it down. It could have been worse because there was serious consideration given to changing FTP-NEA's name to the Sunshine State Education Association. With adequate financing secured, FTP-NEA developed viable programs, member services, and a degree of statewide influence.

In 1978, State Senator Bob Graham was elected governor of Florida, and FTP-NEA members couldn't have been happier. They were not only intimately involved in his campaign from its inception, but couldn't have helped elect a more honest, conscientious, pro-education person to the statehouse. The story of his election is very dear to my heart, not only because the members of FTP-NEA helped elect a good man to office, but also because he came from way, *way* back in the pack to win the election. Graham was from Carol City, Florida, near Miami, and had graduated from the University of Florida and then from Harvard Law School. His father was a wealthy dairy farmer and former state senator. Graham was elected to the state house of representatives in 1966 and again in 1968, and then was elected to the Florida senate in 1970 and 1974. He ended up being elected to two terms as governor of the state in 1978 and 1982. Of course, he later went on to represent Florida in the U.S. Senate, and was a presidential candidate in 2003 before dropping out of the race.

It was important to get FTP-NEA's political house in order, and a good way to do that was to get on board with a winner in the 1978 gubernatorial election, and get on board early. It was clear that FTP-NEA would have to endorse a Democrat because the Republican candidates were abysmal on education and labor issues, but deciding whom to support proved a little tricky because there were six or seven candidates in the race on the Democrat side of the ledger. Graham wasn't one of them.

In the top tier of candidates for the Democrat primary was Bob Shevin, the state attorney general, a good candidate and the heavy favorite. Also in the race was the Florida secretary of state, Bruce Smathers, the son of former U.S. senator George Smathers. Jim Williams, a wealthy citrus farmer and state senator from Ocala, Florida, rounded out the frontrunners in the field.

The sentiment within FTP-NEA was to endorse Bob Shevin. I pushed hard to *not* endorse Shevin if we could find another equal or better candidate to support. FTP-NEA needed its own candidate to support because Shevin was already the heavy favorite and had a truckload of political and organizational endorsements. Much more important to me, at least, was the fact that FEA/U, with much fanfare and media hoopla, had already endorsed him.

Politicians always remember those who were with them early, and endorsing Shevin's campaign after FEA/U's endorsement would have put FTP-NEA at the end of the political queue at the very time FTP-NEA needed to carve out a political niche for itself. We couldn't wait at the end of the line; we needed to take cuts. Debbie DeLee, a former Illinois teacher and local association staff member for the Broward Classroom Teachers Association (Ft. Lauderdale), had just been hired as FTP-NEA's political director. I had a lot of confidence in Debbie, and she agreed totally with my assessment (maybe that's why I had so much confidence in her). Debbie did a wonderful job in Florida, and later became political director for NEA in Washington, D.C.; chair of the Democratic National Committee; and CEO of the Democrat's 1996 convention in Chicago.

There had been some minor speculation about the possible candidacy of Bob Graham, a state senator with an admirable record on education who had had the courage to stand up to the powerful "good ol' boys" from the rural areas of Florida who controlled the state senate. Graham was the perfect candidate as far as education and FTP-NEA were concerned. He was a long shot, but credible, and with FEA/U having already endorsed another candidate, it put FTP-NEA and FEA/U in head-to-head competition.

Graham was also wealthy, always a good attribute for a political candidate. We contacted Graham and asked for a meeting, to which he agreed. Carl Harner, Debbie DeLee, and I met Graham for breakfast at the old Capital Hilton Inn in Tallahassee, just down the street from the state capitol.

We asked him if he would consider running for governor, and he said that he had given it a little thought, but that he had no organization outside of Miami, and that there were already six or seven candidates in the race. We told him that if he would run, we felt certain FTP-NEA would not only endorse him, but would help in any way it could, especially by providing workers in the thirty-three counties we represented. We said that our folks could volunteer, on their own time, to work in his campaign and help with the organizing.

I know that Graham considered a lot of factors in deciding whether or not to run. On the other hand, at that point we were the *only* organization ready to commit time and resources (mostly human resources) to his campaign, and FTP-NEA's prospective support no doubt helped him decide to run. When he announced his candidacy, FTP-NEA endorsed him. Debbie and the rest of us worked tirelessly and effectively in organizing FTP-NEA's campaign on Graham's behalf and coordinated our efforts with Graham's staff beautifully.

All the polls published during the early stages of Graham's run for governor showed that he had about two percent of the Democratic primary vote. Shevin was way out in front, distantly followed by Smathers, Williams, and the others. Right after his campaign began, Graham announced that he would work a different job each day for one hundred days while running for governor. True to his word, he put in a full day's work as a high school teacher, a police officer, a sponge fisherman, a lumberjack, a bellhop, a bus boy, a construction worker, and a garbage collector, to name a few.

The gimmick caught on, and Graham began slowly to rise in the polls. We always figured that if Graham could get into a runoff with Shevin he'd win it, and that's exactly what happened. In the first primary election, Graham received 25 percent of the vote, while Shevin received just over 40 percent. In the runoff election between Shevin and Graham, Graham won with 54 percent of the vote over Shevin's 46 percent. Graham then garnered 56 percent of the vote in the general election against the Republican candidate, Bob Eckerd, a millionaire owner of a drug store chain.

In the general election, Graham carried forty-nine of the sixty-seven Florida counties, and FTP-NEA won right along with him. The organization had backed a winner, one with impeccable education and environmental credentials, and we had gotten into the campaign virtually at the beginning. The victory was satisfying on many different levels, not the least of which was that FEA/U played second political fiddle to FTP-NEA in the election. After Governor Graham assumed office, Debbie DeLee left FTP-NEA to work for the governor on his political staff, and Wally Orr, FTP-NEA's new president, was named by Graham to be Florida's secretary of labor. Wally served in that job for the governor's two full terms.

The most satisfying and rewarding thing to come out of the election was the elation that FTP members all over the state felt. They had worked hard, and they had helped bring home a winner. They wore their "Graham Cracker" lapel pins, stuffed envelopes, worked on telephone banks, labored to get out the vote, and generally brought in as many votes as they possibly could. They got their feet wet politically and achieved positive results for education and teachers, and they liked it. Graham's victory gave Florida an excellent governor who genuinely cared about education.

Also, the FTP-NEA members in Florida began to believe that they could, indeed, make a difference in the political arena. They had suffered through years of segregated schools, they had endured an inferior education system for students, they had participated in a statewide strike that ended badly, and they had seen their state association split in two. Yet in spite of all that, the teachers of Florida continued to teach their students as best they possibly could year after year and never gave up. They had consistently given their all for the education system and the kids they taught, and now they had an ally in the governor's mansion.

Graham turned out to be an excellent governor, and although FTP-NEA didn't always agree with him, and vice versa, the partnership worked just fine. Education was on its way back in Florida, and by the time I left Florida in 1979, FTP-NEA's ship was upright and moving through the water.

CHAPTER 18

Off to Washington

In the spring of 1979, I received a call from Terry Herndon at NEA, who told me that he needed someone in Washington to oversee and coordinate NEA's various program areas, and that he was in the process of creating a new senior-level position for that purpose: NEA assistant executive director. He said it would be operational in late summer and that he would like me to accept the position. I was immediately interested for several reasons: I had been with FTP-NEA for three years and felt that I had accomplished what I had gone there to do.

In those three years the organization had eradicated a $2.5 million debt; purchased and opened its own office building very near the state capital; increased its membership by 30 percent; hired its own staff; established a viable political operation, including a key role in the election of Bob Graham as the state's governor; and built a strong relationship between the state association and its locals.

FTP-NEA had also established a solid reputation with the Florida state legislature and achieved parity with FEA/U in the media. It had been an arduous and demanding job, but virtually everything in the organization was running pretty smoothly, including its governance and administration. I was proud of those accomplishments and keenly aware that it was only a question of time until circumstances would change, probably for the worse. In other words, it was a perfect time to leave—while on top—a philosophy I've always tried to follow.

So it was off to Washington, D.C., to become the NEA assistant executive director under Terry Herndon. For some time, Terry had been considering hiring someone at the senior level to oversee and coordinate

the various programs and personalities within NEA's divisional structure, and several of his executive staff were encouraging him to do so.
When I reported for work, Terry told me there were two things he
needed right away. First, he wanted to know why we could not get a vote
in Congress on a federal collective-bargaining law, one of NEA's top
legislative priorities. He had become terribly frustrated with NEA's inability to help push a bill out of committee year after year. Second, he
wanted to know why NEA had no real access to the staff of the Carter
administration.

Carter was the first presidential candidate NEA had ever endorsed in
its 119-year history. The same organizational philosophy that kept
teachers out of unionism and collective bargaining had applied to electoral politics: such activities were deemed by NEA to be seen by the
public as "unprofessional." As a result, politicians who had no accountability to a teacher constituency were making political decisions
every day about education and teaching.

Although the organization had an excellent relationship with both
Carter and his vice president, Walter Mondale, the absence of con-
nectivity between NEA staff and the White House staff revolved
around a couple of issues. For one thing, key NEA staffers were either inexperienced or unassertive in dealing with the White House.
For another, Carter was a terrible politician. He simply didn't value
the kind of mutually beneficial political connections that every other
president did.

Within a few weeks I split the government-relations operation in
half and established the dual positions of a director of legislation and
a director of political action. I recruited a talented and well-connected
woman in Washington, Linda Tarr-Whelan, for the legislative position.
Tarr-Whelan had been working in the Carter White House and had
previously worked for the American Federation of State, County, and
Municipal Employees (AFSCME) in New York. Tarr-Whelan did an
excellent job for NEA before leaving several years later to head up the
Center for Policy Alternatives (CPA) in town.

I also hired Ken Melley to be the director of political action. Besides
being politically knowledgeable, he had the personality and drive to get
the job done, and he did. Melley soon became one of the premier political action operatives in Washington; everyone knew and respected

him. Melley and Tarr-Whelan made a great team, and NEA's legislative and political programs soared. Terry supported me in all of this without the slightest equivocation.

The lack of interaction between the White House and NEA even extended to the appointment of the nation's first secretary of education. The White House staff never clued NEA in on who was being considered. NEA had sent a name or two to Carter but had heard nothing in return. Finally, when Carter announced that Judge Shirley Hufstedler was to be the nation's first secretary, NEA's response could be summed up in one word: *Huh?* Although they had nothing whatsoever against Hufstedler, neither Herndon nor NEA president Willard McGuire, a genuinely decent man who had succeeded John Ryor as president, was happy about NEA's lack of input into the selection process. Hufstedler was a good, decent judge with little educational expertise. She held her own as secretary, but made little impact.

Aside from the lack of staff contact, what was bothering Herndon most of all was that education was never mentioned in any of the administration's new releases, speeches, or initiatives. Within a week or so after my meeting with Herndon, I attended a Democrat dinner at one of the downtown hotels. Both Carter and Mondale, along with two or three cabinet members, were scheduled to speak. I bought a ticket to the event, and I gnawed on rubber chicken while the program gnawed on me.

Speaker after speaker got up during two hours of political rah-rah. They went on and on about what the Carter administration was doing about a wide variety of topics ranging from the environment, to the economy, to social security. Someone from the association of mayors spoke; someone from county governments spoke; someone from the unions spoke; in fact, someone spoke representing every conceivable aspect of human endeavor in America, *except education*. Not a single word was uttered about education, let alone NEA. Mondale was the penultimate speaker, and he covered the waterfront about the administration's plans and policy priorities, but still not a word about education. Then Carter spoke. Same thing. Unbelievable.

I was dumfounded and upset. Looking back, it seems almost impossible to believe that education wasn't on the politicians' radar screens at that time. I can remember talking to staff from other education organizations, and every one of them was concerned about the same issue. Terry suggested that I contact the only staff person in the White House whom he thought might be helpful, a former educator named Les Francis.

Within a few days after the dinner, I had lunch with Francis. We had quite a lunch, because I was still upset about all of this, and he was the only administration staffer around to whom I could vent. He was very gracious and understanding, and assured me that education was a high priority in the administration; he showed me some talking points on education that he and others carried around with them.

To make a long story short, Francis volunteered to carry the water for education in the White House policy sessions. He also promised to help me establish close working relationships between the NEA staff and key people at the White House. We exchanged names and numbers of key staff people, and that was that. Thanks to Les (who went on to bigger and better things in the Democratic party and private consulting work) things picked up almost immediately. Once I turned matters over to Melley and Tarr-Whelan, Terry didn't have to worry about staff-to-staff connections anymore.

I was also asked to handle coordination between NEA divisions. This task proved more difficult than the others. NEA's large bureaucracy was essentially a classic top-down management structure. Competent, strong-willed, and egocentric division directors vied with each other for turf and prestige. Cooperation between units was spotty at best, and relationships between some division directors were acrimonious. Herndon was a brilliant and insightful leader who had little patience for the day-to-day intricacies of running a bureaucracy. He hired competent, assertive people and expected them to do their jobs. Herndon was not the least bit hesitant to appoint strong-willed, egocentric people to key positions. He wanted competence and performance. He got the former, but not always the latter.

My abilities complemented Herndon's quite well. I was neither brilliant nor charismatic, but I was a hands-on manager who genuinely liked working with people and wouldn't tolerate selfishness or infighting. I've always had a low tolerance for association know-it-alls and independent entrepreneurs. My management philosophy focused on loyalty to the organization, teamwork, cooperation, dissemination of responsibility, and accountability.

For the next four years, until I became executive director in 1983, I worked hard to make those characteristics preeminent in the NEA executive- and management-staff cultures. In the process, I had to get rid of some managers, hire others, and move still others to different positions. I was interested in cooperation and accountability, in getting the job done by communicating and coordinating across unit lines. It was a tough road, but I enjoyed the challenge.

Later, as NEA's executive director, I initiated a comprehensive and dramatic change in the work culture of the NEA staff, all but obliterating top-down decision making, and establishing a system of team responsibility and accountability. The executive and management staff spent countless hours working together to establish the new culture and integrate activities related to program, budget, and staff. The general staff was also an important part of the transitional culture change within the structure. We worked on changing the operational culture for the better part of a decade, with a high degree of success.

In the summer of 1983, the NEA executive committee asked me to apply for the position of NEA executive director to replace Herndon, and I was fortunate enough to get the job. It was a huge challenge for me, but I already knew all the players and had worked with them for the previous four years. In addition to my duties at NEA, I was involved with other educational and progressive organizations, and I served on the boards of directors for Norman Lear's and Tony Podesta's People for the American Way (PFAW), Linda Tarr-Whelan's Center for Policy Alternatives (CPA), and Dorothy Rich's Home and School Institute (HSI).

I genuinely enjoyed my new job, but six years later, in January 1989, Ida died of breast cancer. She was only fifty-one years old and had been courageously battling that awful disease for almost seven years, never once giving up. After Ida's passing, I was glad to be so busy and devoted myself more than ever to the job of trying to improve the lives of school employees.

Over my eighteen years as executive director, I was very much involved in international work with The World Confederation of the Teaching Professions (WCOTP), and was pleased to have played a role in facilitating the merger of WCOTP and the International Federation of Free Trade Unions (IFFTU). The new organization, Education

International (EI), is the largest teachers confederation in the world and does excellent work in the areas of fighting child labor abuse, protecting teachers under political attack, advocating for health issues, and the like.

In the course of my work, I traveled to China, Japan, Russia, Israel, Hungary, all of the European countries, Australia, New Zealand, Central America, Canada, and other places, getting to know teacher-union leaders and comparing education and unions in their countries with those in the United States. I met thousands of wonderful teachers, visited their classrooms, and talked to their students. In Russia, I audited a high school English class where the students had to recite an English sentence first with a British accent and then with an American one. It was a surprise to learn that there are more teachers of English in Russia than there are students of Russian in America.

In Japan, teachers and administrators talked about the Japanese education system and the tremendous pressure put on Japanese students. In Central America, teachers described the political oppression in some of their countries, including the murder of teachers in order to stop their influence. In Hungary, as part of a team sent by the National Democratic Institute (NDI) to monitor the country's first free election in over fifty years, I saw people stand in line for hours to vote and then weep as they cast their ballots.

CHAPTER 19

The Politics of Education

One of the primary reasons for the existence of teacher unions in America is to offset the political nature of the education enterprise. You don't have to be around education very long to realize that it is political from top to bottom and from side to side. Education is an integral part of the American political milieu. Local control of education is one of the fundamental tenets of American education, but even local school-board members run for office and are elected as part of the education/political environment. School-board members, like all politicians, constantly scan the political horizon, and many use their stint on a local board as a stepping-stone to higher office. Jimmy Carter started his political career on a local school board in Georgia, as have countless other political aspirants.

State school boards and superintendents, whether elected or appointed, and state departments of education are political entities greatly affected by the policies and predilections of governors and legislatures. At the federal level, politicians of both parties, whether in Congress or the White House, jostle each other to get their political oars in education's waters. Over the last two decades, education has become one of the very top issues in any election, and politicians watch polls like cats watching birdcages.

During the last thirty-five years, the role of the federal government in education has changed direction frequently, depending on which political party is in office. Lyndon Johnson started the ball rolling when he inserted the federal government into education funding for the first time in any meaningful way by securing passage of the Elementary and

Secondary Education Act (ESEA) in 1965. NEA was very supportive of ESEA, and Johnson addressed the NEA Representative Assembly in New York that year to thank NEA for its help.

Under Johnson, federal school spending went from practically nothing to $16.2 billion. It grew to $28.5 billion under Nixon, and to $32.3 billion under Carter. Reagan took a meat axe to federal spending on education, cutting it back to $27.8 billion, but under President Clinton, education funding increased substantially. President George W. Bush has increased education funding only slightly overall, but NEA got sideways with the administration over its significant shortfall in funding for the No Child Left Behind (NCLB) mandate.

In fact, NCLB, because of its underfunding, has become a financial train wreck for state and local education. While calling for stringent standards to be met by state and local education agencies, it doesn't provide the funding originally promised to implement the law. What was left behind was the money—another federal unfunded mandate.

Consequently, school budgets are in serious jeopardy from coast to coast, and programs are being cut as education experiences yet another political boondoggle. NCLB places tremendous pressure on teachers and students to pass a variety of high-stakes tests. NEA's opposition to the unfunded mandate aspect of the legislation is what prompted Secretary of Education Rod Paige to shamefully call NEA a "terrorist organization." The uncertainty of education funding from one administration to the next is disruptive to the system and harmful to students. Because federal funding for education has atrophied since President Reagan to about 7 percent, and because states are in financial jeopardy, education all over the country is hurting, and the federal government refuses to step into the breach.

The unevenness of federal funding of education has directly reflected the political philosophies of U.S. presidents. After Johnson got the federal ball rolling, Nixon, Ford, Carter (who created the Department of Education), Reagan (who tried mightily to abolish it), Bush, Clinton, and Bush have batted it around like a pinball machine. Nowhere is the federal government's yo-yoing of public education demonstrated more clearly than with the cast of folks who have served as secretaries of education since the department was created in 1979:

Shirley Hufstedler, Terrell Bell, Bill Bennett, Lauro Covasos, Lamar Alexander, Richard Riley, and Rod Paige.

Hufstedler and Covasos were not particularly effective, and seemed to come and go having accomplished little. Terrell Bell was a good man and a solid educator who was directed by President Reagan to get rid of the department of education. Actually, Bell accomplished a great deal while he was in office, communicating effectively with all educators and their organizations and keeping his department's neck away from Reagan's guillotine. He also initiated the *Nation at Risk* report in 1983 that launched a prolonged education-reform era.

As secretary of education, William Bennett was a conservative pedant who used the secretary position as a pulpit to harp on people's moral shortcomings. Bennett always reminded me of a preacher lecturing his congregation about their peccadilloes and threatening them with hellfire. I saw him as a political windbag who criticized education and educators in order to set the stage for his next book. I don't think he actually did anything to help teachers or teaching in any practical way.

Lamar Alexander was a pretty good secretary. Although I didn't agree with some of his ideas, at least he possessed some. He was pro–public education and tried to work with educators and others who cared about public schools. You could talk to Alexander, and he actually listened.

I only met Rod Paige, the current secretary, once or twice when he was superintendent in Houston. I would like very much, however, for Paige to explain why the Houston School District, his own district, produced bogus figures about students' performance and attendance. The district also fiddled with the graduation rates of its students, classifying dropouts as transfer students. Aside from the obvious questions about the integrity of the Houston school administration, it was that so-called "Texas Miracle" that propelled Paige into his job as secretary of education and allegedly served as a model for No Child Left Behind.

When Paige intemperately called NEA a "terrorist organization" in February 2004, he epitomized the politics of public education. He apologized, saying that he was talking about the NEA in Washington, not the teachers it represents. The tactic of differentiating between the organization and its members has never worked.

Richard Riley was, by far, the best U.S. secretary of education. He was honest, straightforward, dedicated to improving education, and genuinely interested in students. He was a great governor in South Carolina, and a dedicated public school advocate. Riley initiated a wide variety of programs and services through the department and never, to my knowledge, engaged in self-serving political confrontation or self-promotion. Not only that, he was genuinely liked by people of all political stripes.

The politics of education is the single most significant reason why educators and their organizations are involved in lobbying and electoral politics. Teachers, more than anyone, know that almost everything that touches them has a string attached that leads to a school board, a legislature, Congress, a mayor, a governor, or an American president. Every school employee contends with that reality every day. Politics in education is far from a new phenomenon, because American education has always been treated like a political Mr. Potato Head.

Never has the political nature of American education been more graphically illustrated than with the release of the *Nation at Risk* report during the Reagan administration. The report was born in the context of the times and became a political ping-pong ball for politicians and reformers to bat around. In the report's aftermath, legitimate efforts to improve education often took a backseat to political spinning and finger-pointing. Education reformers, academics, and politicians lined up to push their philosophies or hawk projects.

For NEA, much of the politics revolved around the U.S. Department of Education. NEA had championed the creation of a separate, cabinet-level Department of Education for over one hundred years, and was jubilant when Congress, with the support of President Carter, established the department in 1979. Teachers looked forward to having education achieve the status and attention from the federal government that it deserved. Those lofty hopes and ambitions came crashing to earth with the election of Ronald Reagan in 1980, less than a year later. Reagan ran for president with the avowed intention of killing the new Department of Education in its crib.

After his election, Reagan was strongly influenced by the right-wingers within his administration who advocated a scorched-earth approach toward public education generally and the department specifically. Understandably, Reagan had trouble finding a candidate for secretary of education who would agree to preside over the abolition of his or her own department and job. Terrell Bell, former state superintendent of schools in Utah, finally agreed to take the position, but from the beginning he sought to mollify Reagan's political agenda regarding public education. He also tried to delay abolition of the Department of Education.

Over the objections of some in his administration, Reagan agreed to convene a prestigious panel of Americans to review the state of American education and issue a blue-ribbon report. Subsequently, a national commission, chaired by David Pierpont Gardner, president of the University of Utah, was formed to accomplish the task. The panel consisted of university presidents, school-board members, school administrators, and a teacher. After eighteen months of deliberation, the commission issued a report that aroused America from its educational torpor more than anything in recent history. *A Nation at Risk* set the condition of America's education in an economic and global context, dramatizing the need for education reform.

The report was well written and had a distinct public relations flair about it. Using analogies to the military, which were no doubt designed to draw media attention, its alarming opening sentence proclaimed, "Our Nation is at risk." The report literally burst onto a fairly placid education landscape and claimed, "The educational foundations of our society are presently being eroded by a rising tide of mediocrity that threatens our very future as a nation and a people."

The report ended with a series of recommendations to the American public including the following: strengthening the curricula and requirements for high school graduation; higher standards for academic performance in schools, colleges, and universities; extension of the school day and year; and increased standards, accountability, and compensation for teachers. It also called for leadership on the part of elected officials to implement the report, and for support from the citizenry at large to hold the elected officials accountable.

Even though much of its data and findings have been challenged by critics, the *Nation at Risk* report threw down the gauntlet for the American people in general, and the education community in particular. It challenged the nation to improve the quality of American education. It was a challenge that deserved everyone's attention and a positive response.

Predictably, the political ping-pong game began immediately, and the first serve came from the president himself. Because the report did not include his pet education issues, Reagan, undaunted, deliberately ignored what *was* in the report and tried to undercut it by championing what was *not* in it. He used the report to call for the abolition of the Department of Education and for school prayer, tuition tax credits, vouchers, and merit pay for teachers.

As NEA's executive director, I essentially liked the report, but not the president's self-serving, political nonresponse to it. Mary Futrell, NEA's newly elected president, publicly supported most of the recommendations in *A Nation at Risk*, and called for the public and the political community to pay heed to its conclusions. Ironically, the report generated so many demands for the federal government to spearhead its implementation that Reagan abandoned his push to abolish the Department of Education. Of course, the fact that he couldn't get the votes in Congress to kill the department also played a major part in his decision.

The *Nation at Risk* report drew attention to public education in a way that virtually no one anticipated, and in dealing with its issues Mary Futrell soon established a reputation as one of the most effective NEA spokespersons in the organization's history. She was deeply committed to kids and education and was willing to take on public education's critics when she thought they were wrong. She also battled some leaders in her own ranks who wanted nothing to do with education reform.

Mary Futrell's personal and professional story is a classic example of the role public education can play in the lives of people who otherwise might not have had a chance at success. In many ways, it personifies the American dream. She grew up with her sister and three foster sisters in a dirt poor, rural environment in the town of Altavista in southern Virginia. The girls were raised by their single-parent mother, Josephine Hatwood, who worked several jobs—cleaning houses, churches, and office buildings—to make ends meet for her extended family.

Ms. Hatwood was a tough taskmaster. When she came home late at night from her last job, she would check the kids' homework, which had to be spread out on the kitchen table. If the homework was incomplete, she would wake up the appropriate girl(s) and make them finish the assignment before going back to bed. The family moved to Lynchberg about the time Mary started school, and her classmates called her

"Seemore," because they said they "could see more holes than material in her clothes." All through elementary school, high school, and college, she attended only segregated schools, where her lack of money and "raggedy" clothing kept her from participating in social events with other students.

When Mary was a senior in high school, several of her teachers urged her to attend college, but she consistently refused to consider it because she could never afford to do so. She didn't know it at the time, but those teachers had gone all over town collecting money to help Mary get her college education. When she went up on the stage at graduation to receive her high school diploma, she was presented with a check for over $1,500, money that the teachers had collected on her behalf. Mary promised her benefactors that she would not only study hard in college, but also become a teacher in order to give back to her community. She has done both.

After graduating from Virginia State University with a teaching degree, Futrell taught business courses at George Washington High School in Alexandria, Virginia. She was elected president of the Alexandria Education Association and later of the Virginia Education Association (VEA). In 1983, she was elected president of the National Education Association and served in that capacity for the next six years. Futrell later became the dean of the Graduate School of Education and Human Development at George Washington University.

The *Nation at Risk* report spread a prairie fire of education reform from coast to coast, and NEA's state and local affiliates found themselves under siege from state legislators and local school boards to support reform activities. They needed help and didn't hesitate to ask NEA for it. Unfortunately, NEA's arsenal of education positions, strategies, and programs had atrophied over the years to the point that the organization was not fully prepared to help them. Governors like Lamar Alexander in Tennessee, Tom Keane in New Jersey, Ray Mabus in Mississippi, Dick Riley in South Carolina, and Bill Clinton in Arkansas were pushing their legislatures for a variety of education-reform measures that directly impacted teachers.

Some governors and state legislatures were hot to impose merit pay on teachers in one guise or another—a real "no-no" for NEA. Some local school districts, like Fairfax County in Virginia, instituted merit-pay plans for teachers with the cooperation of the local NEA affiliates. Other reform initiatives focused on curricula, school choice, teacher testing, teacher training, teacher evaluation, and the elimination of tenure. In Arkansas, Governor Clinton decided to test every teacher in the state in order to determine his or her competence, and engaged in a furious battle with the Arkansas Education Association over the issue.

As indicated earlier, the American Federation of Teachers and Al Shanker approached education reform from a different perspective than NEA. AFT's public initiatives, open-minded rhetoric, and willingness to partner with the business community contrasted glaringly with NEA's "hunker down" posture. Shanker was everywhere offering bold, high-profile education-reform opinions and suggestions, and he garnered a great deal of positive media attention as a result. NEA, meanwhile, was mostly called upon by the media to provide an opposing view to merit pay, which it was more than willing to do. To the organization's dismay, NEA often came across to the public as defending the status quo.

There were, to be sure, some good and significant reform ideas that came to fruition. The concept of establishing a national teachers professional-standards board originated with the Carnegie Foundation for the Advancement of Teaching, which had commissioned a special task force to look into the subject. Futrell and Shanker were both members of the task force, and both endorsed the concept.

Unfortunately, when it came time for the Carnegie task force to issue its final report called *A Nation Prepared*, the NEA executive committee balked. The majority of the executive committee was opposed to the idea of a standards board creating and administering a new category of "master teachers" who would receive additional pay for demonstrated proficiency.

The NEA leaders who were opposed didn't want some teachers to be singled out for special recognition or extra pay. To them, such a designation would have been just a more sophisticated form of merit pay. In fact, a couple of the executive committee members wanted Mary to insist to the task force that before NEA could support the idea of master teachers, all current practicing teachers would have to be grandfathered in—over three million of them. That idea failed in the executive committee, but it was embarrassing. Futrell fought the executive committee tooth and nail to get them to support the standards board, telling them that if NEA opposed its creation, it would be alone and the organization would not be taken seriously on *any* education matters.

Futrell eventually won out, but only because she went over the executive committee's head to the NEA Board of Directors to gain support. Even then, when the Carnegie report was issued in 1986, the NEA executive committee forced Mary to file a minority report putting certain conditions on the establishment of the National Board for Professional Teaching Standards (NBPTS). She filed the minority report, but she ignored the conditions.

NBPTS was created with a majority of classroom teachers on the board. Also on that first board were people like Tom Kean, former governor of New Jersey; James Comer, a professor at Yale; John Gardner, a professor at Stanford; Jim Hunt, former governor of North Carolina; and Futrell and Shanker. The NBPTS is alive and doing very well today, and NEA's support for it has strengthened dramatically.

As if the flames of education reform weren't hot enough, right-wing attacks on teachers, public education, bilingual education, affirmative action, whole-language reading, and teacher unions increased dramatically during the Reagan presidency. It was also during this period that the "school choice" hymn started to be sung, and it didn't take long for a choir to form. While the debates about various education-reform proposals raged, NEA usually raised objections or pooh-poohed many reform proposals. NEA's lack of a positive contribution to the debate was glaringly noticeable, and the organization suffered a self-inflicted wound from which it has never fully recovered.

On the issue of merit pay for teachers, NEA was in a tough spot with the media and the public. Merit pay sounds good and logical on the face of it, yet it is a demonstrably wrongheaded and flawed approach to paying teachers. In the early education-reform days, merit pay became the reform du jour with many state governors and the White House, and NEA affiliates were desperately seeking practical help from NEA to contend with various merit-pay schemes being forced on them.

The NEA executive committee, however, took the position that because merit pay violated NEA's policies, it was wrong for NEA to provide positive assistance on that subject to its own affiliates. Mary and I argued that such a position was not only incorrect, but also irresponsible. NEA existed, we maintained, for the purpose of assisting its members and affiliates. If NEA local affiliates willingly, in cooperation with their school boards, wanted to enter into merit-pay programs and needed NEA assistance, the organization had an obligation to provide it. We stated the obvious: NEA was not violating its own policies by helping affiliates implement theirs.

After one particularly pointed debate on the topic, the executive committee directed me to prevent NEA staff from providing encouragement to affiliates for experimentation, of any kind, with merit pay. I responded that I would instruct staff to refrain from suggesting merit-pay projects or programs to affiliates, but I would not instruct them to refuse to help if the affiliates approached NEA first. It was on that basis that NEA did provide assistance to its local affiliates in Fairfax County, Virginia; Charlotte-Mecklinberg, North Carolina; and several other places.

During these internal debates with the executive committee, I made the case that NEA could engage meaningfully in the public debate on education reform, including merit pay, without violating either its principles or its policies. On the merit-pay issue, for example, I suggested that NEA hold a media conference in which the NEA president would announce that NEA was willing to conduct a restricted merit-pay experiment in equal partnership with a local association, a local school district, a state education agency, and a business company.

When announcing the experiment, NEA would state categorically the specific reasons for its long-standing opposition to merit pay, including chapter and verse about why it has failed every time it has been tried over the last hundred years. However, NEA would say, in spite of its severe misgivings about the efficacy of merit pay, that because there is so much interest in the subject, NEA would be willing to set up the experiment, nurture it, and *keep an open mind* until the results were in. The project would last five years, and at the end of that time the results of the experiment would be judged by a mutually agreed-upon panel of experts employing a mutually agreed-upon evaluation process, and a report would be issued regarding the findings. During the project's five-year duration, NEA, at the national level, would not support other merit-pay schemes.

This kind of approach epitomized for me how NEA could, and should, positively engage in the education-reform debate despite the organization's adamant opposition to some of the ideas being bandied about. It would place NEA in a more positive light and convey that the organization was at least willing to experiment and keep an open mind. Such an approach, I argued, would require no change in NEA policy and—who knows—might turn up something new and worthwhile for consideration.

My suggestion to the executive committee majority crashed and burned like a one-winged airplane. The arguments opposing the idea went along these lines: (1) it's against NEA policy, (2) it won't work, and (3) it would send a signal to merit-pay advocates and politicians that NEA is softening its opposition to an issue of deep concern to its members.

To me, the issue was about NEA being positive instead of negative; it was about trying to help our affiliates even if, at worst, it meant buying time for them; and it was about finding solutions instead of drawing lines in the dirt. I argued that as times and situations change, new approaches to old problems should be considered, and that NEA had an obligation to try new ideas and maybe even retest old ideas. That's a very difficult concept for many union leaders to accept—not understand, but accept. In fairness to the executive-committee members, the merit-pay issue was so clearly unacceptable to so much of NEA that it was politically difficult to get too far in front of them.

However, when people get wedded to a certain way of thinking, they often confuse the activity with the principle (the means with the end). Take collective bargaining, for example. Many local and state teacher-union leaders claim that even to experiment with various alternatives to collective bargaining would be an abandonment of union principles. I've never believed that. Collective bargaining is a strategy, or process, for securing better wages and working conditions for members. The *principle* is to improve salaries and working conditions. The *strategy* is collective bargaining. If standing on one leg and humming Gregorian chants would demonstrably produce the kind of salaries that teachers deserve, I'd stand on one leg and hum myself silly. The only principle I would be violating would be good taste.

Welding a single strategy to a generic principle is daft on the face of it. It hamstrings individuals and organizations from changing with the times, exercising creativity, and engaging in self-renewal. NEA's "don't abandon our principles" true believers will not like the words I have just written any more today than they did in the 1980s, but I believe strongly that an organization not interested in experimentation with new methodologies in order to accomplish a goal is selling itself short. I hasten to add here that the NEA of today is not the NEA of the 1980s. Its attitudes and feelings about education reform have broadened considerably.

However, in the 1980s, the worst part about NEA's lack of positive participation in the education-reform movement was that the country desperately needed the union's positive leadership. Simply saying no to almost everything didn't contribute to a productive environment. NEA's voluntary withdrawal from the field ceded the battle to public education's critics and enemies. During the discussions with the NEA executive committee, I repeatedly pointed out that AFT, specifically Shanker, was gaining significant publicity and credibility while NEA dawdled. I argued that Shanker had it right, not only by assuming a high-profile role in the public debate, but also by offering suggestions for reform.

Although I didn't agree with some of Shanker's comments and proposals, I felt that he took the right path by being publicly open to new ideas and by being positive about the need for systemic school reform; he also engaged education's critics in intellectual, reasoned debate. For her part, Futrell's run-ins with the executive committee and her disdain (at that time) for Shanker and AFT made things difficult for her. Mary later became much friendlier with Al as they found common ground in their international work together.

NEA remained in irons relative to the education-reform debate even after Michigan's Keith Geiger became NEA president in 1989. Keith is a good man, a good friend, and was an effective NEA president. His priorities were collective bargaining, rapprochement with AFT (to his everlasting credit), and building NEA's membership and affiliate base. While Keith accomplished a great deal within the association, it wasn't until Bob Chase's election to the NEA presidency in 1996 that NEA's public image regarding education reform began to change dramatically for the better.

CHAPTER 20

Meritless Pay

For teachers, merit pay is like a recurring nightmare. No matter how many times it has been tried and failed, no matter how many times it has died an ignominious death, merit pay reappears like Michael Myers, the ghoul in the waxen mask who keeps coming back in the never-ending series of *Halloween* horror flicks. A thousand schemes involving merit pay for teachers have been kicked around over the last half-century, and virtually each effort met a disgraceful defeat within a year or two.

First of all, let me define the kind of merit pay I'm talking about: paying additional compensation to some teachers for "superior" teaching (having merit), while not providing that compensation for others. Merit is determined through subjective evaluations by an individual or individuals, such as the building principal or assistant principal, the department head, or whomever.

At first glance, the concept has appeal. After all, the reasoning goes, that's how people in the private sector are paid. Unfortunately, that reasoning is fatally flawed. Teachers are not in the private sector. They do not work for an enterprise that measures success by the bottom line of profit. Teachers, unlike other professionals, are not free to charge whatever the market will bear for their services.

Neither are they free to develop their own curricula, their own methodologies, or their own clientele. Forces outside their control govern the cost of their product—education—as well as their salaries. Comparing teacher pay with other professions or business enterprises is out of kilter because teachers are not in competition with each other.

In their profession, competition with each other is anathema to educating kids effectively.

As sure as you're born, every few years a school board, a school superintendent, a politician, or a public school critic will breathlessly announce a "new" merit-pay initiative for teachers. Here's how the landscape will be painted. The proponents of the latest merit pay scheme will proclaim it to be a fresh and innovative idea—one whose time has come. On cue, a hallelujah chorus of school critics and media pundits will shuffle onto their risers, songbooks in hand, to sing its praises.

Unbelievably, but assuredly, nary a word will be spoken or written about merit pay's abysmal history of failure, including previous plans exactly like the one being proposed. In this vacuum, teachers and their unions will be the only ones to wave a red flag, which will immediately label them as defensive, self-serving, antireform, and intractable. Consequently, their objections will be summarily ignored. It's *Groundhog Day*.

I talked to a District of Columbia School Board candidate some years ago who was promoting a merit-pay plan as part of his campaign. When I pointed out to him that two previous merit-pay plans just like his had been tried within the District of Columbia schools and had failed, his response was revealing. He said that he knew about the previous efforts in the district, but that he needed a hot education-reform issue for his campaign. Besides, he said, who could be against paying good teachers more and bad teachers less!

Merit pay, like virtually everything else in education, is most often a political issue promoted by people who want to make a headline or get a political advantage. I am convinced that most merit-pay advocates don't really care whether it works or not. Imagine the CEO of a major private-sector business being presented by staff with a proposal to improve the company's productivity. The following conversation might occur:

> Staff: This is a great idea, boss. It'll send shock waves through the entire industry.
> CEO: Good, we could use a lift. Has his idea ever been tried it before?
> Staff: Oh, yeah, lotsa times.
> CEO: Has it ever worked?
> Staff: Eh, no.

CEO: Will it improve productivity?

Staff: We don't know.

CEO: Will it save money?

Staff: Only if most of our workers don't have merit.

CEO: Do we know why it failed before?

Staff: Yes, we do.

CEO: Does this proposal correct those faults?

Staff: Eh, no.

CEO: Sounds good to me. Let's go for it.

One of the primary drawbacks of merit pay for teachers is that the evaluation of teacher performance has almost always been subjective and dependent upon the determination of an administrator. The merit-pay trail is littered with the bones of good teachers who were passed over by school administrators who didn't like them, who applied different criteria to different teachers, who applied the same criteria differently to different teachers, or who downgraded teachers whose educational approaches or philosophies differed from their own.

For decades and decades, administrators considered such practices as cooperative education—children working together—to be disorderly. Consequently, innovative teachers were routinely penalized for "lacking discipline in their classrooms." Sometimes obvious personality conflicts between a teacher and the administrator or evaluator—conflicts having nothing to do with performance—caused the teacher to be denied a salary increase.

Most of the merit-pay plans foisted upon teachers over the years have been conceptually flawed or ham-handedly implemented, or both. In the finest tradition of top-down management, teachers were rarely consulted beforehand about the merit-pay plan being imposed upon them; their role was to serve as guinea pigs. Teacher associations or unions were also ostracized from the process, forcing them to react after the fact.

Merit-pay plans for teachers are inherently divisive and disruptive. Some in the private sector find that notion difficult to accept because they live and work in a system that correlates production with financial incentives. Whether one is competing for first chair in a symphony orchestra's violin section or trying to sell more suds for a beer company, competition between individuals and units is encouraged and expected.

A salesperson selling more items than someone else is financially compensated for a higher level of productivity that means profit for the company. Similarly, if a manager within a company contributes leadership and motivational skills that result in bottom-line improvement, that manager is rewarded. Success is plainly quantifiable, and the criteria are objective.

However, private-sector incentives do not apply to the public sector, especially to teachers. Competition between individual teachers for more money has been demonstrated over and over again to be divisive and counterproductive because teachers must work collegially and because there are no objective criteria for measurement. Inevitably, many teachers in a merit-pay system who did not receive a merit-pay increase feel that they worked harder, longer, and more effectively under difficult conditions than some who received an increase. After all, there is no financial bottom line to measure, and every teacher has variables affecting him or her that do not apply to a "competing" teacher. Consequently, teachers in merit-pay systems become disillusioned, their work suffers, and their morale plummets.

However, the biggest problem *by far* with merit-pay plans has been that school districts couldn't, or wouldn't, pay the meritorious teachers as promised. In district after district where merit pay has been implemented, at least some teachers deemed to have merit were stiffed because the school district didn't put up the merit-pay money when the time came. Usually, districts reneged on their commitment because they didn't anticipate that so many teachers would meet their definition of merit. The bottom line is that most merit-pay plans went in the tank because of inadequate funding, and every time another merit-pay debacle occurred, teacher morale plummeted and their (and their union's) cynicism deepened.

Fairfax County, Virginia, a progressive and affluent community just outside Washington, D.C., offers a classic example. In 1989, the school board and the Fairfax Education Association (FEA), an NEA local affiliate, set up a merit-pay plan and did it the right way. The superintendent and teachers, through their association, negotiated the parameters of the merit-pay plan, including criteria for evaluation of teacher performance. The merit-pay idea was originally proposed to FEA by School Superintendent Robert "Bud" Spillane, who assured association leaders that significant funds would be forthcoming if FEA would work with him and the Board of Education to develop and implement such a plan. After much soul-searching, FEA decided to go forward with the plan even in the face of opposition from NEA and many local and state affiliates around the country.

FEA president Mimi Dash and local executive director Rick Willis met with Mary Futrell and me to make sure NEA would not disavow FEA if it went forward, since the plan was a clear violation of NEA's merit-pay policies. We assured them that NEA would not disavow the effort, and I agreed to send NEA staff assistance to Fairfax. Mary spoke to the Fairfax Chamber of Commerce in support of FEA and its willingness to work with the school board. We warned Rick and Mimi that the biggest problem they would face would be to keep the school board from backing out of its commitment to pay the salaries promised. They assured us that the superintendent would stick with it, and they were reasonably sure that the board would also. The plan went forward.

After months and months of cooperative work, the plan went into effect, and many teachers qualified for the merit pay, meeting all the mutually established criteria. In spite of the fact that the plan was executed exactly the way the parties had agreed, the school board cut funding for the meritorious teachers. The school board and FEA had agreed that the merit payments for meritorious teachers would be a 10 percent increase on the salary schedule. When it came time for the first merit increases, the school board *unilaterally* cut the promised 10 percent to 9 percent. Even worse, they unilaterally made it a one-time bonus instead of placing it on the salary schedule. That meant, among other things, that the merit income could not be annually paid as part of salary and that it would not apply to the teacher's retirement calculations.

The second year, the board cut the bonuses fairly severely, and the third year, the board suspended the program. A year later, the board, against the protestations of the superintendent, placed its own merit-pay program before a firing squad and killed it. FEA, feeling justifiably angry and double-crossed, pulled its support for the plan. FEA's willingness to cooperate with the school board on the merit-pay program, against its organizational better judgment, produced the following results: the meritorious teachers were screwed; FEA was screwed; the superintendent was screwed; and teacher cynicism about merit pay deepened throughout the country.

The Fairfax Education Association paid a high price for its merit-pay risk taking. Turmoil within the organization caused membership to drop off significantly (FEA lost over one thousand members in thirteen months; that's as many members as existed in the entire Birmingham, Michigan, teaching faculty back in the '60s). Some members never forgave the association for agreeing to the plan in the first place. While FEA's disastrous venture into the merit-pay swamp is no longer a topic of daily conversation in Fairfax, the organization has still not fully recovered from the fiasco. The association has never regained its previous membership level, and it now has to compete for members with not only AFT, but also with a newly formed organization born as a result of the whole mess.

The idea of merit pay for teachers has an allure that is politically compelling but practically specious. It hasn't worked. It *won't* work — not for teachers anyway. As NEA's current president, Reg Weaver, has said, "Flashy, simplistic remedies will not get the kind of teachers that parents and students need." He's right. However, just as sure as these words are written and you are reading them, another politician will soon breathlessly advocate a *new* merit-pay plan for teachers. The plan may sport a different name or be dressed in different garb, but it will be the same old, reincarnated *Halloween* bogyman, and the horror will begin anew.

CHAPTER 21

NEA and AFT: An Urge to Merge

Keith Geiger was elected NEA president in 1989 after Mary Futrell's tenure. Keith is smart, politically shrewd, effervescent, and effective. He came up through the ranks as a teacher in Livonia, Michigan, and later became president of the Livonia and Michigan Education Associations. After serving as MEA president for nine years (1974 to 1983), Keith was elected vice president of NEA.

Upon assuming the NEA presidency, Geiger sought to integrate professional issues, like a national board for professional teacher certification, into collective-bargaining contracts and salaries for school employees. He wanted to build on the education-reform agenda that Futrell had pursued, but he thought it was time to reemphasize bread-and-butter issues within that context. He also had another issue he wanted to take up—merger discussions with AFT.

Ironically, a few weeks after Keith's election, Bob Chanin, Ken Melley, and I were having dinner and discussing education-reform issues. The subject of Al Shanker came up, which led to a discussion of AFT, which led to a discussion of the tremendously negative attitude toward a merger that permeated NEA.

We agreed that the association's informal taboo about discussing a merger within NEA governance bodies was not healthy, especially because public schools and teacher unions were under severe attack. In that context, it made no sense whatsoever that NEA and AFT were still fighting each other. We decided that it was time to see if we could get the issue of a merger with AFT debated within NEA governance. I said I'd talk to Keith about it, which I did the next day.

Geiger was already ahead of us and had decided to take the political risks necessary to get the ball rolling. We assumed that AFT would be receptive to an invitation from NEA to begin talks because during the 1980s Shanker had sent two (that I know of) informal feelers to Futrell suggesting merger discussions. The offers were not reciprocated, largely because NEA generally, and Mary particularly, were unhappy with Shanker because of statements he had been publicly making about education-reform issues.

Years later, Mary and Al became key players in the merger of the two different international organizations to which NEA and AFT belonged. NEA was a member of the World Confederation of the Teaching Professions (WCOTP), and AFT belonged to the International Federation of Free Teachers Unions (IFFTU). At that time of the international merger, Mary was president of WCOTP, and Al was President of IFFTU. The new, merged organization they helped create was named Education International (EI); Mary became its first president, and Al was designated one of EI's cofounders and EI vice president.

Keith's desire to broach the subject of a merger within NEA came at a good time. The NEA Board of Directors had recently formed a committee to look into what kind of organizational changes NEA should consider as it prepared to go into the twenty-first century. The committee was called the "Special Committee on Organizational Streamlining" and was chaired by NEA vice president Bob Chase. Keith and others lobbied the committee to consider the inclusion of a recommendation to commence merger talks with AFT, and we were pleased when the committee issued its final report and the recommendation about merger talks was included.

After preliminary internal work, including debate within the NEA executive committee (very little), the board of directors (quite a bit), and the representative assembly (lots), NEA was authorized to commence merger discussions with AFT. In approving the merger negotiations, the board of directors and representative assembly made it very clear that NEA's priorities continued as before: no forced affiliation with AFL-CIO, minority representation on all governance bodies, term limits for officers, and secret-ballot elections.

Given the severe cultural differences between the two unions, each of the preconditions was somewhat problematic, but the ban on AFL-

CIO affiliation was a killer because everyone knew that AFT would *never* abandon AFL-CIO. On the other hand, this was a different time, a different place, and a different set of circumstances.

Although few NEA people expected the discussions to be fruitful, it was agreed by most that nothing was possible if the two parties weren't talking. Keith's initiative with NEA governance took a lot of political courage because so many NEA leaders were rabidly opposed to any kind of close relationship with AFT or AFL-CIO. Geiger sent an invitational letter to Shanker, AFT accepted, and NEA-AFT merger discussions began in the fall of 1993.

Most NEA leaders at the affiliate level like the theory of merger, and they love the concept of teacher unity, but they expect a merger to occur only on NEA's terms. Some leaders' attitude toward a merger is to allow AFT to come into the organization—as long as it conforms to NEA's precepts and rules. In other words, they want an absorption, not a merger.

A merger makes sense because, despite the animus between the two organizations, the philosophies and activities of NEA and AFT have become very compatible over the years. Both organizations hold to the same principles regarding the education of children; both are active in legislative and political affairs; both are assertive in advocating for their members; and both are unions, even though NEA is not part of organized labor (AFL-CIO).

Interestingly, NEA became more like a union after the passage of the state collective-bargaining statutes, and AFT became more like a professional association after the release of the *Nation at Risk* report. Today, with the exception of affiliation with organized labor, there are relatively few significant differences between the agendas of NEA and AFT. To be sure, there are myriad cultural differences that distinguish each organization—some of them even acute—but those differences are nowhere near insurmountable.

The merger discussions, led by Keith, got under way in 1993. The first merger session was a historic and exciting occasion, and I couldn't have been more delighted. Both sides fielded good negotiating teams, and both sides negotiated in good faith. AFT named seven people to its negotiating team: Al Shanker, AFT president (chair); Ed McElroy, AFT secretary-treasurer; Phil Kugler, AFT assistant to the president for Organization and Field Services; Tom Hobart, president of the New York State Union of Teachers; Sandy Feldman, AFT vice president and president of New York City's United Federation of Teachers; Nat LaCour, AFT vice president and president of the United Teachers of New Orleans; and Loretta Johnson, AFT vice president and president of the Baltimore Paraprofessionals Union.

NEA also named seven people to its team: Keith Geiger, NEA president (chair); me, NEA executive director; Evelyn Temple, NEA assistant executive director for affiliate services; Sybil Connally, NEA Board of Directors member from Illinois; Ernie Therrien, NEA Board of Directors member from Massachusetts; Jeff Wright, former president of FTP-NEA in Florida; and Linda Day, president of the Louisiana Education Association.

The difference in the political composition of the two teams spoke volumes about the differing political cultures of the two organizations. AFT's team comprised heavy hitters within their organization. They all represented power bases in their own rights, and they were all loyal to Shanker. They all had their own opinions and expressed them, but if and when crunch time came, everyone knew that Shanker would lead the way and the others would follow. It is a large advantage to go to the bargaining table knowing that you can count on your colleagues to follow your lead.

That was by no means the case with NEA's team. Both Keith and Bob Chase, his successor, appointed teams that deliberately, and necessarily, represented a cross section of NEA's political, geographical, affiliate, governance, staff, and racial considerations. Even more problematic was the fact that not everyone on NEA's team even supported the idea of a merger.

Sybil Connally, for example, came from Illinois, a state that opposed an NEA-AFT merger from the beginning to the end of the negotiations. While Sybil tried to keep an open mind, it would have been politically difficult for her within the Illinois Education Association if she actively supported a merger. The bottom line was that neither Keith nor Bob could count on unconditional support at crunch time from all of their colleagues on the negotiating team.

Nevertheless, the NEA and AFT negotiating teams got along well through even the nastiest debates and disagreements. For the most part the issues that divided the two sides became largely organizational rather than personal, and I was genuinely surprised at how quickly everyone put aside previously held animosities. For example, I had a big problem with Tom Hobart from New York because of his self-serving actions during the New York merger twenty years earlier. I never let my personal feelings interfere with what was going on at or away from the negotiating table, but it was hard for negotiators on both sides to tamp down years and years of animus and conflict.

As the leader of AFT's team, Shanker's gregarious nature was in full flow. He was firm about his positions, but at the same time creative and bold in offering suggestions for solution and compromise. Al was given to high abstractions, usually lengthy, about union history, education philosophy, and theoretical constructs. He was clearly a visionary, and there was a kind of utopian symmetry to his long-windedness that we all found fascinating.

Most of the time, however, when Al launched his oratorical fireworks, I pushed my pause button until the outpouring subsided. During the merger discussions, he was fighting the cancer that finally took his life in 1997. Al attended and participated in almost every negotiating session even though he was in obvious discomfort. It got so bad on a few occasions that he had to lie down on a couch away from the table while the talks continued. Even then, however, he paid attention to everything that was going on and never withdrew from the debate.

Geiger, for his part, was ebullient, smart, cocky, honest, and direct. He was an excellent leader who by nature didn't like unproductive meetings, and he absolutely hated wasting time during them. The discussions between the two teams were substantive and often heated, but no matter how intense they got, humor and laughter were always at the ready. Keith had a sense of humor that, while engaging, sometimes made people's eyes roll up to the top of their heads. I used to tell Keith that his sense of humor had been arrested somewhere around the fifth grade. Of course I told my nun joke over and over until thoughts of my strangulation were verbally expressed.

Despite good-faith efforts and positive relations between the NEA and AFT teams, after eighteen months of hard work and numerous negotiating sessions, the discussions broke down in December 1994. The talks failed because we just weren't getting anywhere on vexing issues like AFL-CIO affiliation, term limits for officers, and how to handle incompatible membership categories (AFT has members outside public school settings, while NEA has no such members). When the talks ended, both teams were genuinely disappointed. The good news was that much healthier relationships had developed between at least some of the NEA and AFT leaders. I felt bad that Keith's goal of achieving merger during his presidency was unfulfilled.

Merger talks got cranked up again in 1997 when Bob Chase, NEA's new president, jump-started them. Chase was deeply committed to a merger, and brought a new intensity to the renewed talks. His relationship with Sandy Feldman, AFT's new president, was exceptional. The two teams returned to the table with a freshened determination to find a way to merge the two organizations. Feldman, who succeeded Al Shanker as AFT president after his death, headed AFT's team, and Chase chaired the NEA team. Both groups added a few people to the previous teams, and the talks got off to a good start and pretty much continued down a positive path. The teams met numerous times and hammered out tentative solutions to many of the problems that had hounded them previously.

The NEA Representative Assembly had given its team a certain amount of wiggle room on the issue of AFL-CIO affiliation, so the teams put their collective minds together to find a creative solution to that long-standing issue. The NEA and AFT teams made concessions on several issues, including AFL-CIO, minority representation on governance bodies, and a creative way to handle term limits for officers.

As the talks got progressively more productive, it was agreed that if the parties could reach agreement we would go to our respective conventions with a document of merger "principles" that would do two things if approved by the representative assembly: (1) agree that merger could go forward on a conceptual basis pending the development of governance documents and (2) authorize the drafting of an appropriate constitution, bylaws, and policies for the new, merged organization.

In other words, before arguing over details, both sides needed to know, especially NEA, if their governing bodies would approve the *concepts* that had been negotiated. The decision to present the NEA Representative Assembly with a set of "principles," instead of having every *T* crossed and *I* dotted, may have been a strategic error in retrospect, although it probably wouldn't have mattered. In any event, in the summer of 1998, both NEA and AFT went to their conventions with an agreed-upon set of "Principles of Unity." In that document, virtually all the issues separating the two organizations were conceptually resolved.

NEA and AFT negotiators were proud of their accomplishment, and AFT's leaders were confident that the document would be adopted by their convention. NEA's leaders, on the other hand, were only guardedly optimistic and worried. We couldn't feel confident, because the ratification process was laborious, and there was anything but unanimity among the affiliate leaders and representative assembly delegates.

Quite the contrary, negative reactions were coming from several states, among them Illinois, Michigan, New Jersey, and some of the southern state affiliates. The members of the NEA negotiating team and the executive committee worked diligently to convince state and local affiliate leaders to support the document and encourage their representatives to the 1998 representative assembly in New Orleans to approve it, but it was not to be.

The 1998 NEA Representative Assembly in New Orleans, Louisiana, turned down the merger proposal overwhelmingly (it needed a 2/3 majority, but didn't even get half). The forces arrayed against the merger document were better organized than we had anticipated, and they outmaneuvered the NEA leadership. I was particularly devastated and angry about the rejection for a number of reasons. Much of the tenor of the debate was unnecessarily ugly as some opponents attacked Chase personally. Some local and state affiliate leaders recounted old AFT battle scars like enemy flags displayed on the sides of World War II fighter planes.

The vocal opposition created such a negative climate that the majority of delegates, unsure of whether the speculations and accusations had any truth to them, decided to maintain the status quo and vote against the principles. Some of the merger opponents exploited old fears and prejudices in order to create doubt and uncertainty. They implied that NEA negotiators had abandoned NEA to AFT, just like the state leaders did in New York and Florida two decades earlier. To a degree, their organizational paranoia was understandable because in both New York and Florida, when the smoke cleared, the previous NEA affiliates had adopted AFT's union model.

As ridiculous as it sounds, many affiliate leaders were afraid that the 1-million-member AFT would swallow the 2.5-million-member NEA, and that supporters of the merger document were gullible sheep being led to the slaughter. Some of the rationale offered for rejection of the proposal was disappointing. Some states, like Michigan, opposed a merger because they didn't want to have their organizing activities against AFT and other AFL-CIO unions curtailed.

In other words, they wanted to continue fighting other unions in order to win elections and get more members. Some individuals opposed the merger because they weren't guaranteed a leadership position in the new organization equivalent to what they currently held in NEA (those were the kinds of details that would have been addressed in the governance documents that were to follow adoption of the principles).

I felt that many delegates were more interested in preserving their own organizational status than in unifying the two organizations. More understandable were concerns expressed by some opponents that were clearly organizational in nature rather than personal or self-serving. For example, some state affiliates were concerned about the impact of admitting huge AFT urban locals into their state governance and staffing structures. The political realities within state associations would have been tremendously disrupted if AFT locals like Boston, Chicago, or Detroit had suddenly become part of each state's new, merged organization.

There were three state associations (Minnesota, Montana, and Florida) that were on the brink of merger at the state level and needed affirmation from the representative assembly in order to proceed, and the proposed merger document would have accomplished that objective. Even with the defeat of the merger, however, the representative assembly and board of directors did make the policy modifications necessary to allow the state mergers to proceed. Those mergers only proved once again that if the participants want to get the job done, no obstacle is insurmountable. If the will to merge isn't there, however, any excuse will do.

The failure of the merger agreement in 1998 was by far the biggest disappointment of my NEA career. Bob, Keith, and many others had similar feelings. In spite of my disappointment, however, I've always had tremendous faith in the collective wisdom of the NEA Representative Assembly, and I respect and accept its decision regarding the merger. A merger between NEA and AFT at the national level is now a distant prospect at best because the necessary trust levels between the top leaders of the two organizations won't occur again anytime soon. Geiger, Chase, and I are no longer on the scene, and the commitment of the current NEA leadership to a merger is not as high as it needs to be. Also, it will take some time for wounds to heal after the 1998 merger defeat.

Having said that, the merger discussions from 1993 to 1998 indirectly produced three merged NEA and AFT state affiliates, and others will probably follow in the years ahead. The precedent has been set, and the impetus for local and state organizations to stop fighting with their AFT counterparts and join forces will continue. The quest for an NEA-AFT merger is a tractor pull rather than a stock car race.

CHAPTER 22

New Unionism

At the conclusion of Keith Geiger's term in office, Bob Chase was elected NEA president at the 1996 NEA Representative Assembly. He defeated NEA's secretary-treasurer, Marilyn Monahan, who had been a very popular and effective NEA officer, but who found it exceedingly difficult, as any candidate would, to defeat an incumbent NEA vice president ascending to the presidency. Chase started out as a middle school teacher in Danbury, Connecticut, and became president of the Danbury Education Association and then of the Connecticut Education Association. He was elected to the NEA executive committee in 1985 where he served for four years during Mary Futrell's presidency.

In 1989, Bob was elected NEA vice president and served for the seven-year duration of Keith Geiger's presidency (Keith served an extra year in office because the NEA constitution had been changed to allow the president and other officers to serve two three-year terms instead of three two-year terms). I worked closely with Bob for all the years he was with NEA. He was very knowledgeable about NEA, its programs, its policies, and its politics. As president he was studious, and he preferred ideas over ritual, and cooperation over confrontation. He was a staunch unionist, but by the time he became NEA president he believed that the organization had marginalized itself by becoming entirely too doctrinaire and reclusive.

Bob wanted NEA to broaden its agenda to focus much more on the education of students, and he felt strongly that NEA needed to involve itself more meaningfully in the debate on quality education and school reform. He realized that a new breed of teacher was entering the profession and believed that they wouldn't continue joining NEA unless the organization became more attuned to their professional well-being. In his campaign for NEA president, Chase repeatedly called for significant change to NEA's approach to education and education reform and proposed that NEA should reach out much more assertively to other educators, reformers, and those in the business community.

His philosophy was music to my ears and balm for my soul, having been advocating a similar approach since the *Nation at Risk* report sixteen years earlier. Chase, however, had his own ideas and was absolutely bold in articulating them internally and externally. He had the use of the bully pulpit and was more than willing to take advantage of it. In fact, Chase's performance as NEA president regarding education issues and a new direction for NEA was nothing short of remarkable. His mission was even more amazing because Bob had traveled almost 180 degrees from his positions as a member of the NEA executive committee during Mary's term of office.

After his election, we spent many long hours discussing the best ways to move his agenda forward. He had become convinced, and rightly so, that NEA was not structured programmatically to do the job he envisioned. It only took me about twenty minutes to see that Chase was very serious about his ideas and was willing to put his neck on the line for them. I made it clear that I would help him in any way possible. Two things occurred early in Bob's term of office that got the ball rolling in the right direction in a big way.

First, we commissioned an outside firm, The Kamber Group, to do an "External Communications Review of the National Education Association." That report, which was published internally in January 1997, was called *An Institution at Risk*, the title playing off the earlier *Nation at Risk* report by the federal government. In detail and in graphic terms, the report admonished NEA to change its emphasis from traditional union activities to those dealing with education and teaching—to be a player and innovator in the education-reform arena. The report was widely distributed throughout NEA and provided a tough critique of NEA's insular organizational style; it also prescribed strong medicine. This outside examination and report was exactly what the organization needed, and it served to provide substantial political lift for Chase's agenda.

The second thing that happened was a powerful speech Bob delivered at the National Press Club in Washington, D.C. The staff labored to get a cynical media to pay attention to the speech, promising reporters and pundits that the new NEA president would have something significant and different to say. This was necessary because much of the media had come to expect the same issues and rhetoric from NEA at virtually every news conference.

Chase didn't disappoint. The speech, titled "The New NEA, Reinventing Teacher Unions for a New Era," was delivered at the National Press Club on February 5, 1997. The reaction was astounding, even to Chase and me, and it marked a real turning point for NEA's new direction. In that speech, Bob said,

> I am not shy about my plans to redirect our great association in big ways. Nor am I naïve about the magnitude of this challenge. Bear in mind that, for nearly three decades now, the National Education Association has been a traditional, somewhat narrowly focused union. We have butted heads with management over bread-and-butter issues—to win better salaries, benefits, and working conditions for school employees. And we have succeeded.
>
> Today, however, it is clear to me—and to a critical mass of teachers across America—that while this narrow, traditional agenda remains important, it is utterly inadequate to the needs of the future. It will not serve our members' interest in greater professionalism. It will not serve the public's interest in better-quality public schools. And it will not serve the interests of America's children, the children we teach, the children who motivated us to go into teaching in the first place.
>
> And this latter interest must be decisive. After all, America's public schools do not exist for teachers and other school employees. They do not exist to provide us jobs and salaries. Schools exist for the children—to give students the very best, beginning with a quality teacher in every classroom.
>
> A growing number of NEA teachers argue that it's not enough to cooperate with management on school reform. Quality must begin at home—within our own ranks. If a teacher is not measuring up in the classroom—to put it baldly, if there is a bad teacher in one of our schools—then we must do something about it.

In his Press Club speech, Chase opened the door for candid discussion of these topics—including teacher competence. In so doing, however, he refused to accept hackneyed shibboleths about teacher competence. I was glad that Bob had publicly broached the subject of incompetent teachers. This is a topic that teacher unions are hesitant to discuss publicly because they fear that admitting that a relative *few* incompetent teachers exist will give impetus to critics who contend that *many* incompetent teachers are in the nation's classrooms.

In a profession of millions, some bad teachers inevitably slip through cracks, but the truth is that the *vast* majority of teachers are competent, and a significant percentage of them are exceptional. Most teachers deeply resent ad hominem attacks on the teaching profession by people who are ignorant about how difficult it is to teach (like the father of one of my students telling me in no uncertain terms that everyone knows that teachers are people who can't get a job in a real profession).

Because of such canards and stereotyping, most teachers want their unions to defend them against these negative generalizations, and so the defensiveness of teacher unions on the subject is understandable. Union defensiveness also springs from the illogical accusation that teacher unions are responsible for the existence of incompetent practitioners. That charge is a classic example of displacement and scapegoating. Neither teachers nor their unions decide who is trained to be a teacher. They don't admit incompetent teachers into the profession. They don't certify a single teacher. They never hire anyone into a school district. They don't evaluate incompetent teachers or keep them on the job. And they don't procrastinate or bungle the dismissal of an incompetent teacher.

Nor are most incompetent teachers in the classroom because teacher unions protect their jobs. While teacher unions protect members' rights, as they should, school boards and administrators frequently rationalize that they can't get rid of incompetent teachers because teacher unions or the collective-bargaining agreement won't allow it. Statements like that are arguments of convenience at best, and they cover up the real issues: inattentive hiring practices; inadequate supervision; shoddy or nonexistent evaluation of performance; and, most of all, an unwillingness on the part of many school administrators to confront bad teachers.

School administrators frequently shuffle bad teachers from one post to another or provide them with a good recommendation if they agree to resign. Why is this the case? One reason is the constant pressure on school districts, particularly in urban areas, to supply teachers for their classrooms. Another is that when it comes time to fire or discipline a bad teacher, supportive documentation doesn't exist. In all too many instances, when a teacher is to be fired for incompetence, there are absolutely no written records of negative evaluations; nor has the teacher ever been told that anything was wrong with his or her performance. Hard to believe, but true.

Chase courageously and publicly stepped up to the plate with his Press Club speech, and the response by the media and public was almost universally positive. Among NEA affiliate leaders the reviews were mixed, although largely supportive. Again, the true-believer unionists saw the speech as an abandonment of NEA's union obligations and a retreat from its commitment to collective bargaining. They complained that Chase was calling for NEA to abandon its union principles, a patently superficial and erroneous argument. Notwithstanding the caterwauling from some quarters, the majority of state and local leaders, and certainly the vast majority of the NEA membership, applauded Chase's insights. His initiative became known as "New Unionism," and Bob was more than comfortable with that appellation.

New Unionism was much more than an effort to reinvent NEA for public consumption. It was a philosophy that challenged the organization to be more expansive, more open-minded, more tolerant of political and educational differences in education. It preached cooperation and partnerships whenever possible with traditionally unfriendly (or seemingly unfriendly) groups like the business community, the Republican Party, school administrators (both individuals and their organizations), school boards, and the American Federation of Teachers.

New Unionism was about finding ways to help classroom teachers and other school employees with the problems they faced every day. It opened discussion within NEA on such issues as teacher certification, teacher evaluation, peer review, standardized testing, alternative methods of teacher pay (not merit pay), teaching methodology, "choice" within the public school setting, and teacher training—both in-service and pre-service.

Bob didn't get every item on his reform agenda through the NEA political bureaucracy. He did, however, engender quality debate and consideration for every one of his education issues. Opposition to his education-reform initiatives came largely from those who believed strongly that the organization should stick to its union knitting. Some of the opponents to New Unionism later parlayed that opposition into arguments to reject his recommendation to merge with AFT.

One of the first goals of New Unionism was to reach out to the business community. For a variety of reasons, teachers over the previous one hundred years had become quite distrustful and cynical of the business community at large. Many teachers believed that its real interest in education was twofold: to sell their product(s) through the students and to keep local property taxes down. Their bias was deepened substantially by endeavors like Chris Whittle's Channel One, a commercial venture that mandated students in participating schools to watch a twelve-minute current-events video every day, two minutes of which were commercials for clothing, soft drinks, and the like. In return for playing the videos daily, the school district received free video and TV equipment from Channel One. Many school systems, desperate for such equipment, signed up.

On the other hand, it was obvious that many businesses were genuinely interested in improving the quality of public schools. We determined to probe their interest by scheduling a series of twenty or so private meetings with the CEOs of companies like IBM, Kodak, Proctor & Gamble, Bell South, and Wal-Mart. These meetings, attended by Bob and me, proved to be not only beneficial but also enlightening. Interestingly, most of the CEOs had either read or heard Chase's Press Club speech and were eager to talk to him. The meetings led to better relationships between the business community and NEA and generated several joint projects. Chase was a credible representative for NEA and did a good job of articulating his vision for schools and NEA.

Another area that we tackled right away was NEA's relatively sour relationship with school-administrator groups. I had been maintaining relationships for over fifteen years with the heads of the administrator organizations, and most of the time it was a fairly lonely effort. One vehicle available to me was an informal group that met bimonthly called the Forum for Educational Organization Leaders (FEOL). This forum brought together the presidents and executive directors of thirteen national education organizations. Organization presidents, including

NEA's, attended FEOL sessions sporadically at best, but the executive directors attended regularly.

I became friendly with most of the executive directors of the other organizations, even a couple of the more vocal anti-union curmudgeons. The forum had no bylaws, no dues, no program, no staff, and no real structure. It was a seminar, its meetings originally funded by a small grant from the Department of Education, and it was voluntarily chaired by the group's mentor, Harold "Bud" Hodgekinson, a highly respected academic, researcher, and educational demographer. FEOL presented an opportunity for the leaders of various education organizations to meet regularly, exchange ideas, and get to know each other. Occasionally the group would make an aborted attempt to cooperate on some project or activity, but nothing ever came of it because of interorganizational rivalries, lack of funding, and the absence of any financial commitment to FEOL by the participating organizations.

In 1996, however, FEOL executive directors began talking about the need for a more formal arrangement. A few of the leaders, including me, urged the groups to come together to coordinate their activities, combine their resources for certain education and research purposes, and strengthen their relationships with each other. Transforming FEOL from an informal discussion group to a formal organization would involve getting approval from the participating organizations' governance bodies and then adopting a set of bylaws and a dues structure. It also meant having a program that all the organizations could support. From the beginning of the conversations, everyone agreed that the new organization should not become involved in politics, lobbying, or partisan activities. Instead, it would strive to coordinate the resources of the participating organizations for projects and research on certain education issues. Another of its primary functions would be to coordinate the education activities of the individual organizations and improve their relationships with one another.

Gordon Ambach, of CCSSO; David Imig, of AACTE; Anne Bryant, of NASB; Al Shanker, of AFT; and I pushed hard for the creation of the more formal organization. Rebraiding the strands between the education organizations that had come loose during the turbulent and adversarial collective-bargaining years was important. It was especially important for the organizations to pull together because of the constant and distorted criticism of public education prevalent since the *Nation at Risk* report. The new organization, called the Learning First Alliance, was created in 1996 with all of the old FEOL organizations participating except the Council of the Great City Schools. Its members are: American Association of Colleges for Teacher Education (AACTE), American Association of School Administrators (AASA), American Federation of Teachers (AFT), Association for Supervision and Curriculum Development (ASCD), Council of Chief State School Officers (CCSSO), Education Commission of the States (ECS), National Association of Elementary School Principals (NAESP), National Association of Secondary School Principals (NASSP), National Association of State Boards of Education (NASBE), National Education Association (NEA), National Parent–Teacher Association (PTA), and National School Boards Association (NSBA)..

The creation of the Learning First Alliance, and NEA's endorsement of it, was an important step in reuniting the old education family in a contemporary and more appropriate setting. Partnerships and friendships sprang from the alliance. For example, Anne Bryant, executive director of the National School Boards Association, and I helped create, and co-chaired for the first year, an exciting and productive four-year project called the CEO Forum on Education Technology. A Washington group called Infotech Strategies facilitated the project and secured its funding. This endeavor received wide acclaim, including participation by the Clinton White House and the Department of Education, and provided annual research-based assessments of the state of education technology in America's schools. The reports were lauded and highly utilized by school districts and universities all over the country.

The CEO Forum on Education Technology brought together CEOs from many of the leading technology companies in America, including Apple, IBM, Hewlett-Packard, Bell South, Dell, Compaq, Sun Microsystems, Elextronics International, Verizon, Gateway, and the like. Anne and I looked around the room at the multimillionaire CEOs and thought that many of them could still be in their "Dad, can I have the keys to the car" years. One of the most valuable outcomes of the project was to focus attention on the fact that many teachers had not been trained adequately in the kinds of technology that their students needed to know. The project ended after its original four-year charge.

CHAPTER 23

The Quest to Privatize Education

My quarrel is not with critics who seek to improve public education, but rather with critics who want to destroy it. Many of the latter care less about the *performance* of public education than they do about its very *concept*. They don't believe in public schools in the first place; they don't like them, don't want them, and don't want anyone else to want them.

Some folks believe that public schools are inherently corrupt because they expose their children to ideas, concepts, philosophies, and standards that are different from their own. I am not referring here to racists who want to keep their kids away from minorities. I am referring, for example, to those who recoil from public education because they consider the schools cauldrons of godlessness and immorality. When such parents send their children off to school, they want them encapsulated within a kind of moral and religious bubble.

A subgroup of this crowd peeps through classroom windows in search of teachers promoting witchcraft, Satanism, hedonism, humanism, communism, evolution, bad language, homosexuality, sexual perversion, open-mindedness, tolerance, and other perceived evils. They hear messages from the devil in records and tapes played backward; they find demonic references between the lines of books such as *Harry Potter*; they even find evil messages embedded in the animated clouds or forests of children's movies. To these people, the public schools are part of an anti-God conspiracy conjured up by John Dewey and his hordes of incubi to teach (gasp!) secular humanism.

I've talked to many of these people over the years, and while their fears are irrational, they spring from genuine concerns for their children. Some parents view the public school environment as a threat to the religious values being taught in their home. That's possible, particularly for people like those described above, because America's public schools reflect the broad values of American society and do not promulgate any specific religious beliefs. They are societal mixing bowls that place students in daily contact with other kids, other beliefs, other races, other cultures, and other values. Their exposure to this wide range of American society enhances their life experiences, abets their socialization, and strengthens their character. Their exposure to other cultures, beliefs, and values within the public schools is a blessing, not a curse.

The public schools do not, and should not, advocate any particular religious orthodoxy. For those who feel public schools are a curse rather than a blessing, religious schools may be the answer. After all, they exist for the purpose of inculcating students with the kind of religious education that some parents want. Private and parochial schools provide a viable alternative for people who are threatened by public education or who simply believe that the quality of the education provided is better. Well, one might ask, if public schools exist to provide an education for all students, and private and parochial schools exist to provide a particular religious or educational option for some parents, what's the problem?

The problem is that some people want much more than just the option of a private education for their kids. They want private and religious school "choice," a clever marketing term, but terrible public policy. The very word *choice* implies that parents have no choice but to send their children to public schools, which is not true on the face of it. Everyone can choose to send their children either to a public school or to a private or religious one. What choice proponents want is to be able to send their children to private or religious schools and *be subsidized by public tax dollars*. They want you and me to pay for their religious schools.

Advocates for choice toss out a variety of rationalizations for tax-supported private education. One of the most deceptive of these rationalizations is that school choice will bring about competition between public and private schools, thereby forcing public schools to become better. The argument goes that public education will not reform itself, and tax supported private and religious schools will make public schools restructure and improve. But, taking already insufficient tax dollars away from financially strapped public schools and then demanding that they do a better job of competing with private schools is just loopy. It won't happen. What *will* happen is that private and religious schools will end up educating the best students while the public schools are expected to do more with less money and poorer students.

There are two primary reasons that public funding of private schools, including religious schools, is bad for America. First, it is of primary importance to this country's well-being that the wall of separation between church and state is preserved. Throughout human history, when religion and government have commingled, the country has ended up with bad government *and* bad religion. Look at England during the Reformation, Spain and other European countries during the Inquisition, the Crusades of the Middle Ages, the Salem witch hunts right here in America, the more recent religious/nationalist atrocities in India, or the excesses of most fundamentalist Muslim states.

When America was being fashioned, some, like Thomas Jefferson, advocated a system of secular education separated entirely from religious education. Jefferson was keenly aware of the historically abusive entanglements between church and state in England and other countries. He was very familiar with the high levels of intolerance and oppression that theocracies had imposed on people. Other American patriots, like Patrick Henry, thought that good government and good citizenship were inseparable from Christianity.

Consequently, Henry saw the correct path to democracy as an education system wherein Christian educators would teach their students both academics and Christianity. Jefferson wanted to erect a wall between church and state; Henry wanted to construct a bridge. Jefferson and others had the foresight to see America as a repository for a wide range of religious views, cultures, and philosophies *outside* government. That foresight has served America very well indeed.

The second reason public funding of private schools is wrong is because private schools and religious schools are free to admit or retain whomever they wish—and teach whatever they wish. They don't have to adhere to the same standards that public schools do. If private schools choose to reject admission to some students because their parents are not wealthy enough, they can. If they refuse admission to some students because they aren't smart enough, they can. If they choose to teach that trickle-down, supply-side economics is the only viable economic philosophy, they can. Similarly, religious schools are free to teach students a particular religious creed. They can adhere to restrictive moral codes prohibiting dancing, rap music, reading *Harry Potter*, or whatever. Any and all of these things are acceptable for private and religious schools, but not if the public is paying for it through their tax dollars.

The converse of private education's being free to teach particular religious or social philosophies is that the public schools should not be forced to do the same. It is just plain wrong for citizens to demand that a particular book that has been authorized by a teacher or school system be banned. It is similarly wrong to insist that a particular religious view of God should be taught in the public schools. A Muslim or Jewish youth has a right not to have Christianity promulgated in their public schools. Christian students, likewise, have a right not to be indoctrinated about Islam or Judaism in their public schools. It's not God who is missing from the public schools, it's a particular religion.

NEA has *always* stood squarely for the separation of church and state, and I hope it always will. NEA doesn't oppose school vouchers and choice because it opposes religious or private education. It opposes vouchers or tax credits because it doesn't believe that public tax dollars should be used to support private education. That's why NEA supports groups like People for the American Way, and Americans United for the Separation of Church and State.

CHAPTER 24

Some Thoughts about the Future

No one has all the answers for restructuring American public education to make sure it will serve our nation well and efficiently in the twenty-first century. However, America needs and deserves a better, modernized, education system if it is to meet its future responsibilities domestically and internationally. One thing is for sure: education in this country cannot rise to the level it must achieve if we just tinker around the edges of education reform. The following do not necessarily represent NEA positions; they are mine. Here are a few things that could be a big help.

DROP THE INDUSTRIAL MODEL AS THE BASIS FOR PUBLIC SCHOOL OPERATIONS

The industrial model remains, to this day, the overarching structure for public education and is the single biggest stumbling block to meaningful education reform in America. There are numerous reasons the outdated and debilitating industrial education model should be shelved. First of all, the archaic business philosophy upon which it is premised no longer reflects how private-sector businesses work in modern America. The industrial model will not allow public education to adapt quickly enough to the demands of modern society: the technology revolution, the globalization of the economy, the need for higher-order skills in both the military and business, and the need for a better-educated work force.

The biggest problem of all with the industrial model is that most of the high-wage, low-skill manufacturing jobs in this country, upon which the industrial model is predicated, are gone—poof. Every day, more and more manufacturing and services jobs are either being eliminated or shipped to other countries. The products on America's shelves today could have been manufactured anywhere in the world, and the telemarketing calls we receive can be coming from Indiana or India.

Businesses today are more diversified and technologically oriented than ever and require employees with higher-order skills to do their jobs. In other words, because the economic ground has shifted and the job market has changed radically, the old 85:15 percent ratio for educating American students is antiquated and counterproductive. In order to get good-paying jobs today, young people need to be better educated and more technologically literate than ever before.

In order to meet these new imperatives, systemic, fundamental reform of the *entire system* of public education is needed—from the way schools and school boards are structured, to the way schools are funded, to the way teachers work and the salaries they make, to the curricula being taught. Systemic education reform, however, does *not* mean toying with merit pay, obsessing over standardized tests, using public tax dollars to support school choice, or advancing a new reading program.

Part of the industrial model that has to be jettisoned is the practice of allowing teachers to have the least to say about teaching and learning. That's dumb. What the public schools need is transformational change directed at putting educational expertise in the hands of the practitioners. The teaching staff, including building principals, should make decisions about how best to educate the students in their charge once educational standards are established. Whatever the new system would look like, site-based decision making should be part of it.

In that context, school principals should *truly* function as team leaders and facilitators, not middle managers relaying instructions from corporate headquarters. Many principals already try to function as true team leaders, but the corporate superstructure above the building level hamstrings them, and the lack of resources at the building level frustrates them. Teams at the school level should be given adequate planning time and the help they need to be successful, and they should plug into the latest research and thinking about education. Local sites should also be responsible for determining teaching methods, textbook selection, and administration of the school budget. And, *with that kind of support*, that's exactly where the accountability for the education product should be focused: at the school-building level.

The problem with achieving true systemic reform is that many layers of bureaucracy have to come together to reach consensus: teachers, administrators, school boards, legislatures, governors, teacher unions, and parents. Even more important, because politics permeates every aspect of education, and because citizens of every community in America have a financial stake in quality education, transformational change can't be accomplished solely by school districts. The federal government, particularly the president of the United States, has to take the lead in pulling all this together, and *Congress must fully fund the work*.

TAKE A LOOK AT THE STRUCTURE OF SCHOOL BOARDS

As part of the systemic change needed for public schools, the structure and function of local school boards must be part of the equation. Their primary function, to ensure the quality and effectiveness of education, is atrophying, especially in the big cities. School-board members have too often become appallingly political, paralyzing the board with internal bickering and power grabs. In the large cities in particular, politics in education is becoming *more* chronic, not less.

Between 1995 and 2000, twenty-eight school districts were taken over by city or state governments, and since 2000 it has happened in New York, Philadelphia, and Prince George's County (Maryland). The mayor of Washington, D.C., is now threatening to do the same there, notwithstanding the fact that the D.C. school board has been taken over before. Having mayors or legislatures take over school boards is not the answer; that's simply a case of one political fish swallowing another, especially if the mayors then appoint their political friends or cronies to school-board positions. In those instances, the new school board simply becomes part of the mayor's political apparatus, and the board sinks even lower into the political quicksand.

One salient approach is the idea of a caucus system for appointing school-board members, something along the lines of what exists in Cleveland, Ohio, and Boston, Massachusetts. In Cleveland, the board of education is made up of nine members appointed by the mayor to four-year terms, but the mayor can only appoint individuals who are nominated by a community-based "nominating panel." The all-volunteer nominating panel reviews applications from people who want to serve on the board. The panel then makes recommendations for three applicants for each open seat, and the mayor must select one of those three.

The nominating panel is diverse and is made up of eleven volunteer members selected as follows:

- Three parents or guardians of children attending the Cleveland schools appointed by the district PTA or similar organization se-lected by the state superintendent of public instruction
- Three people appointed by the mayor
- One person appointed by the president of the Cleveland city council
- One teacher appointed by the collective-bargaining representative of the district's teachers
- One principal appointed through a vote of the district's principals
- One representative of the business community appointed by an organized-business entity selected by the mayor
- One president of a public or private institution of higher education located within the district appointed by the state superintendent of public instruction
- At any given time, four of the nine board members must have demonstrated before their appointment that they possess signifi-cant expertise in one of three fields: education, finance, or business management.

This system makes sense and accomplishes several important goals. It keeps citizens involved in the selection process and also involves the mayor, the business community, the teachers and their union, the school administration, the city council, and higher-education faculty. Best of all, it establishes some criteria for serving on the board of edu-cation, and a panel of community members receives and reviews ap-plications from *any* citizen of the school district who would like to be on the board, then winnows the applications down to three people for each vacant position. The panel makes those recommendations to the mayor, who must then select one of the three for each position. Now what's wrong with that? Evidently, not much, because the plan went into effect in 1998, and the citizens of Cleveland reconfirmed the plan by a large margin in 2001.

The National School Boards Association (NSBA) is doing some excellent work in trying to refocus school boards on their mission "to raise student achievement and engage the community in attaining that goal." Through several venues, including its comprehensive Key Work program, NSBA is working hard to educate school-board members about their contemporary roles as stewards of the system and leaders of their community. The difficulty they face is that they function in a highly charged, political environment, one infused with society's economic and cultural problems.

PROVIDE MORE FUNDING FOR PUBLIC EDUCATION FROM THE FEDERAL LEVEL

The federal government today contributes only a small percentage of the money spent on education (7 percent or less), while state and local communities shoulder about 93 percent of the cost. Conservatives frequently complain that the billions of dollars spent on public education at the local, state, and national levels is already excessive. They claim that throwing money at education's problems won't solve them. When that assertion is brandished by legislators who are not the least bothered by pork-barrel politics involving their own constituents, the claim borders on calumny.

The truth is that this country has *never* thrown money at public education, not the kind of money it will take to get the job done. Spending the money it would take to educate 100 percent of America's youth to be high-skilled workers would be an investment that would pay rich dividends for the nation's economy and productivity. It would also narrow the alarming and increasing disparity between high- and low-paying jobs. American society would be the beneficiary.

It is incontrovertible that the proper education of American students is vital to the *national* interest. This commonsense declaration was affirmed by the U.S. Supreme Court in 1923 (*Meyer v. Nebraska*), when it stated, "The American people have always regarded education and the acquisition of knowledge as matters of supreme importance." Later, in *Brown v. Board of Education*, the Supreme Court reaffirmed that idea, stating that education "is required in the performance of our most basic public responsibilities. It is the very foundation of good citizenship."

The national interest of an educated, productive citizenry is at least as important as national defense, and it can't be supported on the cheap. Because there are 50 million students to educate in the public schools of America, and because the public interest in an educated citizenry doesn't disappear when it crosses a state boundary, the federal government must shoulder the lion's share of the funding for this national imperative.

Some critics want public schools to receive *less* money, not more. They expect a quality education for every student while ignoring the awe-inspiring magnitude of the task. They recognize and appreciate the importance and complexity of the military budget because they appreciate the size of the enterprise and recognize its vital importance to national security. In that regard, they are more than willing to accept a degree of bureaucracy and inefficiency. Yet they get apoplectic at perceived inefficiencies in the public school enterprise. When inefficiencies exist in an area of vital national interest, like defense and education, the way to deal with those inefficiencies is to correct the problem, not deny the vital importance of the national interest.

Think what could be accomplished for the lower 85 percent of the American student population if the president and Congress took the $87 billion initially approved for the reconstruction of Iraq and spent it for the reconstruction of American education. Just think what could be accomplished if every American kid who needed extra reading or math help got that help. What if children who came to school from dysfunctional families got special help with their studies? What if class sizes were *significantly* reduced? Doing so would actually ensure that virtually *every* student could read proficiently by the end of the third grade and compute proficiently by the seventh grade.

From state to state and local community to local community, school funding is politically vulnerable, uneven, unequal, and unpredictable. In most cases, it is also inadequate. Further, the profoundly changing nature of student enrollments plays havoc with the educational process. Another rationale for federal funding is that the federal government can engage in deficit spending, while many state constitutions prohibit them from doing so, even in times of financial stress. Compared to other developed nations, America's funding of its public schools is out of whack. According to John D. Donahue in *The Case for Serious Federal Financing of America's Public Schools*, in OECD (Office for Economic Cooperation and Development) countries approximately 55 percent of the funding for primary and secondary education comes from the central governments. Regional governments contribute 26 percent, and local governments 22 percent.

ADOPT A NATIONAL CURRICULUM AND BASIC STANDARDS

America should set national standards and establish a national core curriculum. This idea goes against the grain of states'-rights absolutists and some segments of the anti–federal government people, but come on! Americans from coast to coast should have the same educational focus and goals. The national curriculum would be a core curriculum established at the national level with the participation of the federal, state, and local governments.

The standards would not force states that might have higher standards to cut back, but the current hodgepodge of state standards (some of which have little relevance to what is being taught) are not producing the desired result for America—and they won't until all American students have the same core curricula, all school districts have the same goals, and all districts are responsible for the same education.

The national curricula would not be a Christmas tree of pedagogical and political ornaments, nor would it be unilaterally dumped on already beleaguered states. The curricula would also be accompanied with the funding necessary to help the students meet the standards. Why not have a national curriculum that says that all students must be appropriately educated in English, mathematics, science, and history (left to my own devices, I'd throw in geography too)?

Setting benchmarks for student achievement would be necessary, but how to achieve those results would be left to local communities to decide. There is no reason why local control of education should be affected in any negative way, and every local school district would have the benefit of knowing that certain core subjects, and the standards that go with them, are applicable in every community throughout the country.

There is no reason for a national curriculum to affect local control of education. School boards would be free to supplement or enrich their programs; decide on methodology for curriculum delivery; organize schools; hire, fire, transfer, and evaluate teachers; develop pay schedules; and so on. A national curriculum, in short, would not take over public education at the local level.

PAY TEACHERS MORE MONEY

Teacher pay is still lousy, especially when compared to other professions. According to the census and NEA data, here are the figures for 2002:

Lawyers	$77,100
Engineers	$72,400
Accountants	$52,300
Teachers	$41,800

In some states the beginning salary for teachers is still only about $23,000. In many places throughout this country, teachers have to work two jobs to make ends meet. The turnover rate among young teachers is way too high, and many of these teachers are leaving the profession because they can't afford to remain.

A recent story in the *Washington Post* about the difficulties facing low-income teachers in high-income communities quoted one twenty-three-year-old teacher in Alexandria, Virginia, who said that she makes about $2,000 a month as a teacher and $400 a month working other jobs. "It all goes to pay rent and groceries," she said. Then she went on: "Being a teacher, you really don't get professional respect." (Sound familiar?) She said she was reconsidering her career choice even though she enjoys teaching. If we want to get the best and brightest into America's classrooms, and if we are going to keep them there, we have to find a way to pay teachers the kind of money they deserve.

That is extremely unlikely to happen in this country as long as the local property tax remains the foundation for funding schools and paying the salaries of their employees. The U.S. Constitution is silent on where the responsibility for funding education rests (understandable, since public schools did not emerge until long after the Constitution was adopted).

However, it is becoming increasingly clear that the federal government must place education at a level of priority similar to the military, and it must *substantially* augment the funds available at the local and state levels for quality education and quality teacher pay. Not much can or will change if state and local communities are forced to continue providing almost 95 percent of school funding.

STOP THE UNFUNDED MANDATES

State and federal governments have a long history of passing legislation that mandates public schools to do one thing or another, or teach this or that, or test everything that moves. In and of itself, that's a big problem. One of the biggest headaches for local school districts is when the government at one level or another legislatively imposes an education program on a district and then refuses to provide funds to implement it. This forces the schools to comply with the legislation even though they don't have the money to do the job. Local school districts are left holding the financial bag. A good example at the national level was the passage in 1975 of Public Law 94-142, the Education of All Handicapped Children Act (now called the Individuals with Disabilities Education Act, or IDEA).

That legislation mandated that students with learning disabilities be "mainstreamed" into America's classrooms. While educationally desirable, that program caused great anxiety among classroom teachers who were not trained to teach these previously special-education students. An even bigger problem was that full funding did not accompany the legislation. The education community was largely left to fend for itself, and it took years for school systems to get their feet on the ground.

Another example is President Bush's "No Child Left Behind" legislation, formerly known as the Elementary and Secondary Education Act (ESEA). This legislation imposes standards for learning achievement on the public schools, including penalties if goals are not met. Educators all across America are reeling from the standards themselves and the rigid time lines that accompanied them. The real cause for alarm is the lack of simultaneous federal funding to help states and local school districts meet the imposed deadlines. In fact, many states are rebelling, and both Republicans and Democrats are critical of the way the initiative has been handled by the administration.

Unfortunately, unfunded mandates are not just a federal problem. State legislatures are prone to the same approach, leaving the problem of funding for local school districts to handle. The impact of all this on lower-income communities, already suffering budget shortfalls and program cuts, is disastrous.

ENOUGH ALREADY WITH THE STANDARDIZED TESTS

This country has gone bananas with high-stakes standardized testing. The most consistent complaint from teachers today is the preoccupation of federal and state governments with high-stakes testing. There is so much testing going on that teachers are losing more and more of their teaching time with students, and many teachers feel that the kids are so busy preparing for standardized tests that they aren't getting the time they need for other important educational priorities—like learning and thinking.

There is mounting evidence that the proliferation of standardized testing has had unintended negative consequences for students. Two recent studies by the Education Policy Studies Laboratory at Arizona State University for the Great Lakes Center for Education Research and Practice shed some light on what teachers have long known. Audrey Amrein, coauthor of the reports along with David Berliner, says, "The impact high-stakes and high school graduation exams have on academic achievement is, at best, ambiguous. Contrary to popular thought, high-stakes tests do not increase academic achievement."

One study shows that high-stakes tests might actually inhibit the academic achievement of students. The other study found increased dropout rates and lower graduation rates in sixteen states with high-stakes graduation exams. More and more teachers are "teaching to the test" by making sure that students learn what is sure to be tested, and drilling them on facts and working with them on test-taking strategies. There's an old adage that says, "You can't fatten a sheep by weighing it"; neither can we educate kids by constantly testing them.

When I visited Japan fifteen years ago and talked to school administrators and teachers there, they told me that they wished their education system was not so rigid, and they looked to the United States as having the right approach to testing. They don't have the same feeling about the American model today. Teachers in this country spend all their time getting ready to give tests, teaching to the tests, or actually administering them. America's rush toward standardized testing turned into a stampede with Bush's No Child Left Behind scheme. It should have been called "No Test Left Behind."

That's my wish list. I'm not naïve enough to believe for an instant that things will change much in the near future; without question, most things will go on as before. Teachers will continue to be undervalued and underpaid, the federal government will not treat public education as a significant national responsibility, and the grenadiers of privatization and school choice will continue to throw their bombs at the wall that separates church and state in this country. The changes recommended here are neither insignificant nor temporary; they are transformational in nature and almost overwhelming in scope. But they, or something else systemically significant, must come—for the good of the nation.

Index

About the Author

Born in Detroit, Michigan, **Don Cameron** was educated in Michigan's public schools, earned his bachelor's and master's degrees in education at Eastern Michigan University, did postgraduate work at the University of Michigan and New York University, and was awarded an honorary doctorate by Eastern Michigan University. He taught English and history at the secondary level in Birmingham, Michigan, before embarking on a long and varied career with the National Education Association, culminating in his tenure of executive director from 1983 to 2001.

Cameron was instrumental in the creation of the Learning First Alliance, a broad consortium of twelve national education organizations, and cofounded the CEO Forum for Education Technology, a business/education partnership between the CEOs of twenty high-tech companies, the NEA, and the National School Boards Association. He has received numerous honors and awards, including the Presidential Citizen's Medal, awarded by President Clinton, the highest national award given to an American civilian. He is also a charter member of the Eastern Michigan University Education Hall of Fame and has received an honorary fellowship from the Education Institute of Scotland, granted under a royal charter. He has been a member of the board of directors of many organizations, including People for the American Way, CEO Forum for Education Technology, Learning First Alliance, Education Commission of the States (ECS), NEA Foundation for the Improvement of Education, Princeton Review, Center for Policy Alternatives, National Democratic Institute for International Affairs (NDI), United Nations Association, Home and School Institute, and American Arbitration Association. Don Cameron lives in Arlington, Virginia.